LITERATURE FROM CRESCENT MOC

Sexing Hardy: Thomas Hardy and Feminism
by Margaret Elvy

Thomas Hardy's Jude the Obscure: A Critical Study
by Margaret Elvy

Thomas Hardy's Tess of the d'Urbervilles: A Critical Study
by Margaret Elvy

Stepping Forward: Essays, Lectures and Interviews
by Wolfgang Iser

Andrea Dworkin
by Jeremy Mark Robinson

German Romantic Poetry: Goethe, Novalis, Heine, Holderlin
by Carol Appleby

Cavafy: Anatomy of a Soul
by Matt Crispin

Rilke: Space, Essence and Angels in the Poetry of Rainer Maria Rilke
by B.D. Barnacle

Rimbaud: Arthur Rimbaud and the Magic of Poetry
by Jeremy Mark Robinson

Shakespeare: Love, Poetry and Magic in Shakespeare's Sonnets and Plays
by B.D. Barnacle

Feminism and Shakespeare
by B.D. Barnacle

The Poetry of Landscape in Thomas Hardy
by Jeremy Mark Robinson

D.H. Lawrence: Infinite Sensual Violence
by M.K. Pace

D.H. Lawrence: Symbolic Landscapes
by Jane Foster

The Passion of D.H. Lawrence
by Jeremy Mark Robinson

Friedrich Holderlin: *Selected Poems*
translated by Michael Hamburger

Rainer Maria Rilke: *Selected Poems*
translated by Michael Hamburger

Walking In Cornwall
by Ursula Le Guin

The North Sea

THE NORTH SEA

HEINRICH HEINE

Translated by Emma Lazarus
Edited and Introduced by Carol Appleby

CRESCENT MOON

CRESCENT MOON PUBLISHING
P.O. Box 1312, Maidstone
Kent, ME14 5XU
Great Britain
www.crmoon.com

First published 1881. This edition 2017.
© Carol Appleby 2017.

Printed and bound in the U.S.A.
Set in Book Antiqua 11 on 14pt.
Designed by Radiance Graphics.

The right of Carol Appleby to be identified as the editor of this book has been asserted generally in accordance with sections 77 and 78 of the Copyright, Designs and Patents Act 1988.

British Library Cataloguing in Publication data

Heine, Heinrich
The North Sea. – (European Poets Series)
I. Title II. Lazarus, Emma III. Appleby, Carol IV. Series
305.4201

ISBN-13 9781861715692

CONTENTS

A NOTE ON THE TEXT

The poems in *The North Sea* are taken from *Poems and Ballads*, translated by Emma Lazarus, published by R. Worthington, New York, NY, 1881.

Heinrich Heine

Heinrich Heine

THE NORTH SEA

1825-26

TO

FREDERICK MERCKEL

THE PICTURES OF

THE NORTH SEA

ARE AFFECTIONATELY DEDICATED BY THE AUTHOR

THE NORTH SEA

FIRST CYCLE

To be disinterested in everything, but above all in love and friendship, was my supreme wish, my maxim, my practice; hence my daring expression at a later period: 'If l love thee, what is that to thee?' sprang directly from my heart.

Wolfgang von Goethe's *Truth and Poetry*, Book xiv

I. CORONATION

Oh songs of mine! beloved songs of mine,
      Up, up! and don your armor,
    And let the trumpets blare,
        And lift upon your shield
          This youthful maiden
        Who now shall reign supreme
      Over my heart, as queen!
Hail! hail! thou youthful queen!
        From the sun above
      I snatch the beaming red gold,
    And weave therewith a diadem
      For thy consecrated head.
From the fluttering azure-silken canopy of heaven,
    Where blaze the diamonds of night,
    A precious fragment I cut:
    And as a coronation mantle,
    I hang it upon thy royal shoulders.
      I bestow on thee a court
      Of richly-attired sonnets,
Haughty *Terzine* and stately stanzas.
      My wit shall serve thee as courier,
      My fancy shall be thy fool,
Thy herald, whose crest is a smiling tear,
      Shall be my humor.

      But I myself, oh Queen,
      Low do I kneel before thee,
    On the cushion of crimson samite,
And as homage I dedicate to thee.
      The tiny morsel of reason,

That has been compassionately spared me
  By thy predecessor in the realm.

II. TWILIGHT

On the wan shore of the sea
Lonely I sat with troubled thoughts.
The sun dropped lower, and cast
Glowing red streaks on the water.
And the white wide waves,
Crowding in with the tide,
Foamed and rustled, nearer and nearer,
With a strange rustling, a whispering, a hissing,
A laughter, a murmur, a sighing, a seething,
And amidst all these a mysterious lullaby.
I seemed to hear long-past traditions,
Lovely old-time fairy-tales,
Which as a boy I had heard,
From the neighbor's children,
When on summer evenings we had nestled
On the stone steps of the porch.
With little eager hearts,
And wistful cunning eyes,
Whilst the grown maidens
Sat opposite at their windows
Near their sweet-smelling flower pots,
With their rosy faces,
Smiling and beaming in the moonlight.

III. SUNSET

The glowing red sun descends
    Into the wide, tremulous
    Silver-gray ocean.
Ethereal, rosy tinted forms
Are wreathed behind him, and opposite,
Through the veil of autumnal, twilight clouds,
    Like a sad, deathly-pale countenance,
      Breaks the moon,
    And after her, like sparks of light,
In the misty distance, shimmer the stars.

    Once there shone forth in heaven,
      Nuptially united.
Luna the goddess, and Sol the god.
And around them gathered the stars,
    Those innocent little children.

But evil tongues whispered dissension,
      And in bitterness parted
      The lofty, illustrious pair.

      Now all day in lonely splendor
The sun-god fares overhead,
Worshipped and magnified in song,
    For the excellence of his glory,
By haughty prosperity-hardened men.
      But at night
In heaven wandereth Luna,
      The poor mother,
With her orphaned, starry children;
And she shines with a quiet sadness,

And loving maidens and gentle poets
Dedicate to her their tears and their songs
Poor weak Luna! Womanly-natured,
    Still doth she love her beautiful consort.
    Towards evening pale and trembling,
She peers forth from light clouds,
And sadly gazes after the departing one,
And in her anguish fain would call to him, "Come!
Come! our children are pining for thee!"
    But the scornful sun-god,
    At the mere sight of his spouse,
      Glows in doubly-dyed purple,
      With wrath and grief,
And implacably he hastens downward
To the cold waves of his widowed couch.

* * *

Thus did evil-whispering tongues
    Bring grief and ruin
    Even upon the immortal gods.
And the poor gods in heaven above
    Painfully wander
Disconsolate on their eternal path,
    And cannot die;
And drag with them
    The chain of their glittering misery.

But I, the son of man,
The lowly-born, the death-crowned one,
    I murmur no more.

IV. NIGHT ON THE SHORE

Starless and cold is the night,
    The sea yawns;
And outstretched flat on his paunch, over the sea,
    Lies the uncouth North-wind.
Secretly with a groaning, stifled voice,
Like a peevish, crabbed man in a freak of good humor,
    He babbles to the ocean,
And recounts many a mad tale,
    Stories of murderous giants,
    Quaint old Norwegian Sagas,
And from time to time, with re-echoing laughter,
    He howls forth
The conjuration-songs of the Edda,
    With Runic proverbs
So mysteriously arrogant, so magically powerful,
That the white children of the sea
High in the air upspring and rejoice,
    Intoxicated with insolence.

Meanwhile on the level beach,
    Over the wave-wetted sand,
Strides a stranger whose heart
    Is still wilder than wind or wave.
    Where his feet fall
Sparks are scattered and shells are cracked.
And he wraps himself closer in his gray mantle,
And walks rapidly through the windy night,
    Surely guided by a little light,
That kindly and invitingly beams
    From the lonely fisherman's hut.

Father and brother are on the sea,
  And quite alone in the hut
  Bides the fisher's daughter,
The fisher's rarely-beautiful daughter.
  She sits on the hearth,
And listens to the cosy auspicious hum
  Of the boiling kettle,
And lays crackling faggots upon the fire.
  And blows thereon,
  Till the flickering red flames
  With a magic charm are reflected
  On her blooming face.
On her delicate white shoulders
  Which so pathetically outpeep
  From the coarse gray smock,
  And on her little tidy hand
Which gathers more closely the petticoat
  About her dainty loins.

But suddenly the door springs wide,
  And in steps the nocturnal stranger
  His eyes rest with confident love
  On the slim, white maiden,
  Who stands trembling before him,
  Like a frightened lily.
And he flings his mantle to the ground
  And laughs and speaks.
"Thou see'st my child! I keep my word.
  And I come, and with me, comes
The olden time when the gods of heaven
  Descended to the daughters of men,
  And embraced the daughters of men,
  And begot with them
  A race of sceptre-bearing kings,

And heroes, the wonder of the world.
But thou my child, no longer stand amazed
At my divinity.
And I beseech thee, boil me some tea with rum,
For it is cold out doors,
And in such a night-air as this,
Even we, the eternal gods, must freeze.
And we easily catch a divine catarrh,
And an immortal cough."

V. POSEIDON

The sunbeams played
Upon the wide rolling sea.
Far out on the roadstead glimmered the vessel
That was to bear me home.
But the favoring wind was lacking,
And still quietly I sat on the white down,
By the lonely shore.

And I read the lay of Odysseus,
The old, the eternally-young lay,
From whose billowy-rushing pages
Joyously into me ascended
The breath of the gods,
And the lustrous spring-tide of humanity,
And the blooming skies of Hellas.

My loyal heart faithfully followed
The son of Laertes in his wanderings and vexations,
By his side I sat with troubled soul,
On the hospitable hearth
Where queens were spinning purple.

And I helped him to lie and happily to escape
From the dens of giants and the arms of nymphs.
And I followed him into Cimmerian night,
Into storm and shipwreck,
And with him I suffered unutterable misery.

With a sigh I spake: "Oh, thou cruel Poseidon,
Fearful is thy wrath,
And I myself tremble

For mine own journey home."
Scarce had I uttered the words,
When the sea foamed,
And from the white billows arose
The reed-crowned head of the sea-god.
And disdainfully he cried:
"Have no fear, Poetling!
Not in the least will I imperil
Thy poor little ship.
Neither will I harass thy precious life
With too considerable oscillations.
For thou, Poetling, hast never offended me.
Thou hast not injured a single turret
On the sacred stronghold of Priam.
Not a single little lash hast thou singed
In the eyelid of my son Polyphemus;
And never hast thou been sagely counselled and protected
By the goddess of wisdom, Pallas Athene."

Thus exclaimed Poseidon,
And plunged again into the sea.
And, at his coarse sailor-wit,
Laughed under the water
Amphitrite, the stout fish woman,
And the stupid daughters of Nereus.

VI. DECLARATION

Shadowing downward came dusky evening,
　　Wildly the breakers rolled,
I sat alone upon the shore and gazed
　　At the white dance of the waves.

And my bosom heaved with the sea,
A deep homesickness yearningly seized my heart
　　　For thee, oh lovely image,
　　Who surround'st me everywhere,
　　Who call'st to me everywhere,
　　　Everywhere, everywhere,
In the rushing of the wind, in the dashing of the sea,
　　And in the sighing of mine own breast.

With a slender reed I wrote upon the sand,
　　"Agnes, I love thee!"
But the wicked waves came overflowing
　　That sweet confession,
　　And blotted it out.

Oh brittle reed! oh swiftly-scattered sand!
Oh flowing waves, I trust you no more!
The heavens grow darker, my heart beats more wildly,
And with a mighty hand, from the Norwegian woods,
　　I snatch the loftiest fir,
　　　And I plunge it
　　Into Etna's glowing gulf;
And, with such a fire-steeped giant's pen,
I write on the dusky canopy of heaven,
　　"Agnes, I love thee!"

Each night hereafter overhead shall blaze
   Those eternal letters of flame.
And all future generations of our descendants
   Shall joyously read the celestial sign,
     "Agnes, I love thee!"

VII. NIGHT IN THE CABIN

The ocean hath its pearls,
The heaven hath its stars,
But oh, my heart, my heart,
My heart hath its love.

Great are the sea and the heavens,
But greater is my heart.
And fairer than pearls or stars
Glistens and glows my love,

Thou little, youthful maiden,
Come unto my mighty heart.
My heart, and the sea, and the heavens
Are melting away with love.

* * *

On the azure vault of heaven,
Where the beauteous stars are shining,
I am fain to press my lips now,
Wildly press midst stormy weeping.

Yonder myriad stars the eyes are
Of my darling, and they twinkle,
And they beckon to me kindly
From the azure vault of heaven.

Towards the azure vault of heaven,
Towards the eyes of my beloved,
Piously mine arms uplifting,
Thus I supplicate and worship;

Lovely eyes, ye lights of heaven,
Graciously my soul inspire
Let me die and let me win you,
You and all your spacious heavens.

* * *

From the eyes of heaven yonder,
Golden sparks fall trembling downward,
Through the night. My soul dilateth,
Filled and overfilled with passion.

Oh ye eyes of heaven yonder,
Weep yourselves to death within me!
Till my spirit overfloweth
With the radiant starry tear drops.

* * *

Cradled by the waves of ocean,
And by drowsy thoughts and visions,
Still I lie within the cabin,
In my berth so dark and narrow.

Through the open hatchway yonder,
I can see the stars clear shining.
The beloved eyes so gentle,
Of my gentle well-beloved.

The beloved eyes so gentle
Hold above my head their vigil;
And they glimmer and they beckon
From the azure vault of heaven.

On the azure vault of heaven,
Still I gaze through blessed hours,
Till a white and filmy vapor
Veils from me those eyes beloved.

* * *

Against the wooden wall of the ship
   Where my dreaming head reclines,
Break the waves, the wild sea-waves.
     They whisper and murmur
     Close into mine ear:
   "Oh foolish young fellow,
Thine arm is short and the sky is far off,
And the stars are all firmly nailed above
     With golden nails.
Vain is thy yearning and vain is thy sighing!
The best thou canst do is to go to sleep."

* * *

I dreamed a dream about a strange vast heath,
All overlaid with white and quiet snow.
And I beneath that white snow buried lay,
And slept the cold and lonely sleep of death.
But from the dark and shadowy heavens yonder,
Upon my grave the starry eyes looked down.
Those gentle eyes! Triumphantly they sparkled,
With still serenity, yet full of love.

VIII. STORM

The tempest is raging.
It lashes the waves,
And the waves foaming and rearing in wrath
Tower on high, and the white mountains of water
　　Surge as though they were alive,
While the little ship over-climbs them
　　With laborious haste,
　　And suddenly plunges down
Into the black, wide-yawning abyss of the tide.

　　O sea.
Thou mother of beauty, of the foam-engendered one,
　　Grandmother of love, spare me!
　　Already scenting death, flutters around me
　　The white, ghostly sea-mew,
　　And whets his beak on the mast.
And hungers with glutton-greed for the heart
Which resounds with the glory of thy daughter,
　　And which the little rogue, thy grandson,
　　Hath chosen for his play-ground,

　　In vain are my prayers and entreaties,
My cry dies away in the rushing storm,
　　In the battle-tumult of the winds.
They roar and whistle and crackle and howl
　　Like a bedlam of tones.
　　And amidst them, distinctly I hear
　　Alluring notes of harps,
　　Heart-melting, heart-rending,
　　And I recognize the voice.

Far away on the rocky Scotch coast,
     Where the little gray castle juts out
          Over the breaking waves,
     There at the lofty-arched window
     Stands a beautiful suffering woman,
Transparently delicate, and pale as marble.
     And she plays on the harp, and she sings,
And the wind stirs her flowing locks,
          And wafts her melancholy song
          Over the wide, stormy sea.

IX. CALM

Calm at sea! The sunbeams flicker
Falling on the level water,
And athwart the liquid jewels
Ploughs the ship her emerald furrows.

By the rudder lies the pilot
On his stomach, gently snoring,
Near the mast, the tarry ship-boy
Stoops at work, the sail repairing.

'Neath their smut his cheeks arc ruddy,
Hotly flushed, his broad mouth twitches.
Full of sadness are the glances
Of his eyes so large and lovely.

For the captain stands before him,
Raves and scolds and curses: "Rascal!
Little rascal, thou hast robbed me
Of a herring from the barrel."

Calm at sea! above the water
Comes a cunning fish out-peeping.
Warms his little head in sunshine,
Merrily his small fins plashing.

But from airy heights, the sea-mew
On the little fish darts downward.
Carrying in his beak his booty
Back he soars into the azure.

X. AN APPARITION IN THE SEA

I however lay on the edge of the vessel,
    And gazed with dreamy eyes
    Down into the glass-clear water.
And gazed deeper and deeper,
    Deep down into the bottom of the sea.
      At first like a twilight mist,
Then gradually more distinctly colored,
Domes of churches and towers arose,
And at last, as clear as sunshine, a whole city,
    An antique Netherland city,
      Enlivened with people.
    Grave men with black mantles,
    And white ruffs, and chains of honor,
    And long swords and long faces,
    Strode over the swarming market-place,
Towards the court-house with its high steps,
    Where the stone effigies of emperors
Kept guard with scepter and sword.
    Near by, past long rows of houses,
Past casements like polished mirrors,
    And pyramidal, clipped lindens,
Wandered, in rustling silks, the young maidens,
    With slender forms, and flower-faces
Decently encircled by their black hoods,
    And their waving golden hair.
    Motley-clad folk in Spanish garb
    Strut past and salute each other.
      Elderly dames
In brown, old-fashioned attire,
Missal and rosary in hand,
    Hasten with tripping steps

Towards the great cathedral,
Drawn thither by the chiming bells,
And by the deep-voiced tones of the organ.

And the far-off chimes smite me also
With mysterious awe.
Insatiable yearning, profound sadness
Steal into my heart,
Into my scarcely-healed heart.
I feel as if its wounds
Were kissed open by beloved lips,
And began to bleed afresh,
With hot, red drops,
That fall long and slowly,
On an old house below there,
In the deep city of the sea; –
On an old high-gabled house,
Sadly deserted by all living creatures,
Save that in the lower window,
Sits a maiden,
Her head resting on her arms,
Like a poor, forsaken child,
And I know thee, thou poor forsaken child.
Deep down, deep as the sea,
Thou hiddest thyself from me,
In a childish freak,
And never could'st rise again.

And thou sat'st a stranger among strangers,
Through long ages,
Whilst I, my soul full of grief, –
I sought thee over the whole earth.
Forever I sought thee,
Thou ever-beloved,
Thou long-lost,

Thou found at last!
I have found thee, and I see once more
Thy sweet face,
The wise, loyal eyes,
The darling smile,
And never again will I leave thee,
And I come down to thee now,
And with wide-stretched arms,
I leap down upon thy breast.

But just at the right moment
The captain seized me by the foot,
And drew me from the edge of the vessel,
And cried with a peevish laugh,
"Doctor, are you possessed by the devil?"

XI. PURIFICATION

Remain in thy deep sea-home,
Thou insane dream,
Which so many a night
Hast tortured my heart with a counterfeit happiness,
And which now as a vision of the sea
Dost threaten me even in the broad daylight.
Remain there below to all eternity!
And I cast moreover down unto thee
All my sorrows and sins,
And the cap and bells of folly
That have jingled so long upon my head.
And the cold, sleek serpent's skin
Of dissimulation,
Which so long has enwound my soul –
My sick soul,
My God-denying, angel-denying
Wretched soul.
Hilli-ho! Hilli-ho! Here comes the breeze.
Up with the sails! They flutter and belly to the wind.
Over the treacherous smooth plain
Hastens the ship
And the emancipated soul rejoices.

XII. PEACE

High in heaven stood the sun,
    Surrounded by white clouds.
    The sea was calm;
And I lay musing on the helm of the ship,
Dreamily musing, and, half-awake,
Half asleep, I saw Christ,
    The Savior of the world.
In waving white raiment
    He strode gigantically tall
        Over land and sea.
    His head touched heaven,
He spread his hands in benediction
    Over land and sea;
And for a heart in his bosom
        He bore the sun,
        The red fiery sun,
And the red, fiery sun-heart
    Showered its beams of grace,
And its pure love-bestowing light,
    That illumines and warms
        Over land and sea.
Peals of festal bells drew hither and thither,
As swans might draw by chains of roses
        The smooth-gliding vessel,
And sportively drew it to the verdant banks,
    Where folk dwelt in a lofty-towered
        Overhanging town.
Oh miracle of peace! How quiet was the town!
Hushed was the dull murmur of chattering, sweltering
           Trade.
And through the clean, resounding streets,

Walked people clad in white,
Bearing branches of palm.
And when two such would meet,
They looked at each other with ardent sympathy
And, trembling with love and self denial,
Kissed each other's brow,
And glanced upward
Towards the sun-heart of the Savior,
Which in glad propitiation irradiated downward
Its crimson blood:
And thrice they exclaimed,
"Praised be Jesus Christ!"
Could'st thou have conceived this vision,
What wouldst thou have given,
Most dearly beloved, –
Thou who art so weak in body and mind,
And so strong in faith!
Thou who so singly honorest the Trinity,
Who kissest daily the pug and the reins and the paws
Of thy lofty protectress,
And hastenest with canting devotion
To the Aulic councilor and to the councilor of justice,
And at last to the council of the Realm
In the pious city,
Where sand and faith flourish,
And the long-suffering waters of the sacred Spree
Purify souls and dilute tea.
Couldst thou have conceived this vision
Most dearly beloved,
Thou hadst borne it to the lofty minnows of the market
place,
With thy pale blinking countenance,
Rapt with piety and humility;
And their high mightinesses
Ravished and trembling with ecstacy,

Would have fallen praying with thee on their knees,
    And their eyes glowing with beatitude,
    Would have promised thee an increase of salary,
    Of a hundred thalers Prussian currency.
And thou wouldst have stammered with folded hands,
    "Praised be Jesus Christ!"

THE NORTH SEA

SSCOND CYCLE

Motto, Xenophon's *Anabasis,* IV. V

I. SALUTATION TO THE SEA

Thalatta! Thalatta!
All hail to thee, thou Eternal sea!
All hail to thee ten thousand times
From my jubilant heart,
As once thou wast hailed
By ten thousand Grecian hearts,
Misfortune-combating, homeward-yearning,
World-renowned Grecian hearts.
The waters heaved,
They heaved and roared.
The sun poured streaming downward
Its flickering rosy lights.
The startled flocks of sea-mews
Fluttered away with shrill screams;
The coursers stamped, the shields rattled,
And far out, resounded like a triumphal pæan,
Thalatta! Thalatta!

All hail to thee, thou Eternal Sea!
Like the language of home, thy water whispers to me.
Like the dreams of my childhood I see it glimmer.
Over thy billowy realm of waves.
And it repeats to me anew olden memories,
Of all the beloved glorious sports,
Of all the twinkling Christmas gifts,
Of all the ruddy coral-trees,
Tiny golden fishes, pearls and bright-hued mussels,
Which thou dost secretly preserve
Below there in thy limpid house of crystal.
Oh, how I have pined in barren exile!
Like a withered flower

In the tin box of a botanist,
My heart lay in my breast.
I feel as if all winter I had sat,
A sick man, in a dark, sick room,
Which now I suddenly leave.
And dazzlingly shines down upon me
The emerald spring, the sunshine-awakened spring,
And the white-blossomed trees are rustling;
And the young flowers look at me,
With their many-colored, fragrant eyes.
And there is an aroma, and a murmuring, and a breathing
and a laughter,
And in the blue sky the little birds are singing,
Thalatta! Thalatta!

Thou valiant, retreating heart,
How oft, how bitter oft
Did the fair barbarians of the North press thee hard!
From their large victorious eyes
They darted burning shafts.
With crooked, polished words,
They threatened to cleave my breast.
With sharp-pointed missives they shattered
My poor, stunned brain.
In vain I held up against them my shield,
The arrows whizzed, the strokes cracked,
And from the fair barbarians of the North
I was pressed even unto the sea.
And now with deep, free breath, I hail the sea,
The dear, redeeming sea –
Thalatta! Thalatta!

II. TEMPEST

Gloomy lowers the tempest over the sea,
And through the black wall of cloud
  Is unsheathed the jagged lightning,
Swift outflashing, and swift-vanishing,
Like a jest from the brain of Chronos.
  Over the barren, billowy water,
  Far away rolls the thunder,
And up leap the white water-steeds,
  Which Boreas himself begot
Out of the graceful mare of Erichthon,
  And the sea-birds flutter around,
  Like the shadowy dead on the Styx,
Whom Charon repels from his nocturnal boat.

  Poor, merry, little vessel,
Dancing yonder the most wretched of dances!
  Eolus sends it his liveliest comrades,
Who wildly play to the jolliest measures;
  One pipes his horn, another blows,
A third scrapes his growling bass-viol.
And the uncertain sailor stands at the rudder,
  And constantly gazes at the compass,
  The trembling soul of the ship;
And he raises his hands in supplication to Heaven –
  "Oh, save me, Castor, gigantic hero!
And thou conquering wrestler, Pollux."

III. WRECKED

Hope and love! everything shattered
    And I myself, like a corpse
That the growling sea has cast up,
      I lie on the strand,
      On the barren cold strand.
    Before me surges the waste of waters,
Behind me lies naught but grief and misery;
    And above me, march the clouds, –
The formless, gray daughters of the air,
    Who from the sea, in buckets of mist,
        Draw the water,
      And laboriously drag and drag it,
      And spill it again in the sea –
        A melancholy, tedious task,
      And useless as my own life.

The waves murmur, the sea mews scream,
Old recollections possess me;
Forgotten dreams, banished visions,
Tormentingly sweet, uprise.

There lives a woman in the North,
A beautiful woman, royally beautiful.
    Her slender, cypress-like form
Is swathed in a light, white raiment.
Her locks, in their dusky fullness,
    Like a blessed night,
Streaming from her braid-crowned head,
        Curl softly as a dream
        Around the sweet, pale face;
    And from the sweet pale face

Large and powerful beams an eye,
        Like a black sun.
    Oh thou black sun, how oft,
How rapturously oft, I drank from thee
    The wild flames of inspiration!
And stood and reeled, intoxicated with fire.
Then there hovered a smile as mild as a dove,
About the arched, haughty lips.
    And the arched, haughty lips
Breathed forth words as sweet as moonlight,
    And delicate as the fragrance of the rose.
    And my soul soared aloft,
And flew like an eagle up into the heavens.
    Silence ye waves and sea mews!
        All is over! joy and hope –
    Hope and love! I lie on the ground
        An empty, shipwrecked man,
        And press my glowing face
        Into the moist sand.

IV. SUNSET

The beautiful sun
Has quietly descended into the sea.
The surging water is already tinted
        By dusky night –
But still the red of evening
        Sprinkles it with golden lights.
And the rushing might of the tide
Presses toward the shore the white waves,
That merrily and nimbly leap
Like woolly flocks of sheep,
Which at evening the singing shepherd boy
        Drives homeward.

"How beautiful is the sun!"
Thus spake after a long silence, the friend
        Who wandered with me on the beach.
And, half in jest, half in sober sadness,
        He assured me that the sun
Was a beautiful woman, who had for policy
        Espoused the old god of the sea.
        All day she wanders joyously
In the lofty heavens, decked with purple,
        And sparkling with diamonds;
        Universally beloved, universally admired
        By all creatures of the globe,
        And cheering all creatures of the globe
With the radiance and warmth of her glance.
        But at evening, wretchedly constrained,
        She returns once more
        To the wet home, to the empty arms
        Of her hoary spouse.

"Believe me," added my friend,
And laughed and sighed, and laughed again,
"They live down there in the daintiest wedlock;
Either they sleep or else they quarrel,
Until high upheaves the sea above them,
And the sailor amidst the roaring of the waves can hear
How the old fellow berates his wife:
  'Round strumpet of the universe!
  Sunbeam coquette!
The whole day you shine for others,
 And at night for me you are frosty and tired.'
   After such curtain lectures, –
  Quite naturally bursts into tears
The proud sun, and bemoans her misery,
And bemoans so lamentably long, that the sea god
 Suddenly springs desperately out of his bed,
And quickly swims up to the surface of the ocean,
 To collect his wits and to breathe."

 Thus did I myself see him yester-night,
  Uprise from the bosom of the sea.
  He had a jacket of yellow flannel,
   And a lily-white night cap,
  And a withered countenance.

V. THE SONG OF THE OCEANIDES

'Tis nightfall and paler grows the sea.
And alone with his lonely soul,
There sits a man on the cold strand
And turns his death-cold glances
Towards the vast, death-cold vault of heaven,
And toward the vast, billowy sea.
On airy sails float forth his sighs;
And melancholy they return,
And find the heart close-locked,
Wherein they fain would anchor.
And he groans so loud that the white sea-mews,
Startled out of their sandy nests,
Flutter circling around him.
And he laughingly speaks to them thus:

"Ye black-legged birds,
With white wings, oversea flutterers!
With crooked beaks, salt-water bibbers,
Ye oily seal-flesh devourers!
Your life is as bitter as your food.
I, however, the fortunate, taste naught but sweets!
I taste the fragrance of the rose,
The moonshine-nourished bride of the nightingale.
I taste still sweeter sugar-plums,
Stuffed with whipped cream.
And the sweetest of all things I taste,
The sweets of loving and of being loved!

"She loves me, she loves me, the dear girl!
Now stands she at home on the balcony of her house,
And gazes forth in the twilight upon the street.

And listens and yearns for me, really!
Vainly does she glance around, and sigh,
And sighing she descends to the garden,
And wanders midst the fragrance and the moonlight,
And talks to the flowers, and tells them
How I, her beloved, am so lovely and so lovable – really!
Later in her bed, in her sleep, in her dreams,
Blissfully she hovers about my precious image,
So that in the morning at breakfast
Upon the glistening buttered bread,
She sees my smiling face,
And she devours it for sheer love – really!"
Thus boasted and boasted he,
And meanwhile screamed the sea-mews,
As with cold, ironical tittering.
The twilight mists ascended,
Uncannily forth from lilac clouds
Peered the greenish-yellow moon.
Loud roared the billows,
And deep from the loud roaring sea,
As plaintive as a whispering monsoon,
Sounded the song of the Oceanides
Of the beautiful, compassionate mermaids,
Distinct midst them all the lovely voice
Of the silver-footed spouse of Peleus –
And they sigh and sing:

"Oh fool, thou fool, thou boasting fool,
Tormented with misery!
Destroyed are all thy hopes,
The playful children of the heart –
And ah! thy heart, Niobe-like,
Is petrified with grief!
In thy brain falls the night,
And therein are unsheathed the lightnings of frenzy,

And them makest a boast of thy trouble!
    Oh fool, thou fool, thou boasting fool!
    Stiff-necked art thou as thy forefather,
    The lofty Titan, who stole celestial fire
    From the gods, and bestowed it upon man.
    And tortured by eagles chained to the rock,
Olympus-high he flung defiance, flung defiance and
                 groaned,
    Till we heard it in the depths of the sea,
And came to him with the song of consolation.
    Oh fool, thou fool, thou boasting fool!
    Thou, however, art more impotent still.
'Twere more seemly that thou shouldst honor the gods,
    And patiently bear the burden of misery,
    And patiently bear it, long, so long,
Till Atlas himself would lose patience,
And cast from his shoulders the ponderous world
          Into eternal night."

    So rang the song of the Oceanides,
Of the beautiful compassionate mermaids,
    Until louder waves overpowered it.
    Behind the clouds retired the moon,
        The night yawned,
And I sat long thereafter in the darkness and wept.

VI. THE GODS OF GREECE

Full-blooming moon, in thy radiance,
    Like flowing gold shines the sea.
With daylight clearness, yet twilight enchantment,
    Thy beams lie over the wide, level beach.
And in the pure, blue starless heavens,
      Float the white clouds,
      Like colossal images of gods
      Of gleaming marble.

No more again! those are no clouds!
    They are themselves the gods of Hellas,
Who erst so joyously governed the world,
    But now, supplanted and dead,
Yonder, like monstrous ghosts, must fare,
    Through the midnight skies.
Amazed and strangely dazzled, I contemplate
    The ethereal Pantheon.
The solemnly mute, awfully agitated,
    Gigantic forms.
There is Chronos yonder, the king of heaven;
    Snow-white are the curls of his head,
The world-renowned Olympus-shaking curls.
He holds in his hand the quenched lightning,
    In his face dwell misfortune and grief;
    But even yet the olden pride.
    Those were better days, oh Zeus,
When thou didst celestially divert thyself
With youths and nymphs and hecatombs.
    But the gods themselves, reign not forever;
    The young supplant the old,
    As thou thyself, thy hoary father,

And thy Titan-uncle didst supplant
Jupiter-Parricida!
Thee also, I recognize, haughty Juno;
Despite all thy jealous care,
Another has wrested thy sceptre from thee,
And thou art no longer Queen of Heaven.
And thy great eyes are blank,
And thy lily arms are powerless,
And nevermore may thy vengeance smite
The divinely-quickened Virgin,
And the miracle-performing son of God.
Thee also I recognize, Pallas Athena!
With thy shield and thy wisdom, could'st thou not avert
The ruin of the gods?
Also thee I recognize, thee also, Aphrodite!
Once the golden, now the silvern!
'Tis true that the love-charmed zone still adorns thee
But I shudder with horror at thy beauty.
And if thy gracious body were to favor me
Like other heroes, I should die of terror.
Thou seemest to me a goddess-corpse,
Venus Libitina!
No longer glances toward thee with love,
Yonder the dread Ares!
How melancholy looks Phoebus Apollo
The youth. His lyre is silent,
Which once so joyously resounded at the feast of the gods.
Still sadder looks Hephaistos.
And indeed nevermore shall the limper
Stumble into the service of Hebe,
And nimbly pour forth to the assemblage
The luscious nectar. And long ago was extinguished
The unextinguishable laughter of the gods.

I have never loved you, ye gods!

For to me are the Greeks antipathetic,
　And even the Romans are hateful.
But holy compassion and sacred pity
　　Penetrate my heart,
When I now gaze upon you yonder,
　　　Deserted gods!
Dead night-wandering shadows,
　Weak as mists which the wind scares away.
And when I recall how dastardly and visionary
　Are the gods who have supplanted you,
　　The new, reigning, dolorous gods,
Mischief-plotters in the sheep's clothing of humility,
　Oh then a more sullen rancor possesses me,
　　And I fain would shatter the new Temples,
And battle for you, ye ancient gods, –
　　For you and your good ambrosial cause.
　　　And before your high altars,
　Rebuilt with their extinguished fires,
　　Fain would I kneel and pray,
And supplicating uplift mine arms.

　　　Always ye ancient gods,
　Even in the battles of mortals,
Always did ye espouse the cause of the victor.
But man is more magnanimous than ye,
And in the battles of the gods, he now takes the part
　　Of the gods who have been vanquished.

✳ ✳ ✳

Thus spake I, and lo, visibly blushed
　　Yonder the wan cloud figures,
And they gazed upon me like the dying,
Transfigured by sorrow, and suddenly disappeared.
　　　The moon was concealed

Behind dark advancing clouds.
Loud roared the sea,
And triumphantly came forth in the heavens
The eternal stars.

VII. THE PHOENIX

A bird comes flying out of the West;
    He flies to the Eastward,
Towards the Eastern garden-home,
Where spices shed fragrance, and flourish,
And palms rustle and fountains scatter coolness.
And in his flight the magic bird sings:

"She loves him! she loves him!
    She carries his portrait in her little heart,
And she carries it sweetly and secretly hidden,
And knoweth it not herself!
But in dreams he stands before her.
She implores and weeps and kisses his hands,
      And calls his name,
    And calling she awakes, and she lies in affright,
    And amazed she rubs her beautiful eyes, –
She loves him! she loves him!"
Leaning on the mast on the upper deck,
    I stood and heard the bird's song.
Like blackish-green steeds with silver manes,
Leapt the white crisp-curling waves.
Like flocks of swans glided past,
With gleaming sails, the Helgolands,
The bold nomads of the North Sea.
Above me in the eternal blue
    Fluttered white clouds,
And sparkled the eternal sun,
The Rose of heaven, the fire-blossoming,
Which joyously was mirrored in the sea.
    And the heavens and seas and mine own heart
      Resounded in echo –
She loves him! she loves him!

VIII. QUESTION

By the sea, by the desolate nocturnal sea,
     Stands a youthful man,
His breast full of sadness, his head full of doubt.
And with bitter lips he questions the waves:
"Oh solve me the riddle of life!
The cruel, world-old riddle,
Concerning which, already many a head hath been racked.
     Heads in hieroglyphic-hats,
     Heads in turbans and in black caps,
    Periwigged heads, and a thousand other
    Poor, sweating human heads.
Tell me, what signifies man?
Whence does he come? whither does he go?
Who dwells yonder above the golden stars?"

The waves murmur their eternal murmur,
The winds blow, the clouds flow past.
    Cold and indifferent twinkle the stars,
     And a fool awaits an answer.

IX. SEA-SICKNESS

The gray afternoon clouds
Drop lower over the sea,
Which darkly riseth to meet them,
And between them both fares the ship.
Sea-sick I still sit by the mast
And all by myself indulge in meditation,
Those world-old ashen-gray meditations,
Which erst our father Lot entertained,
When he had enjoyed too much of a good thing,
And afterward suffered such inconvenience.
Meanwhile I think also of old stories;
How pilgrims with the cross on their breast in days of yore,
On their stormy voyages, devoutly kissed
The consoling image of the blessed Virgin.
How sick knights in such ocean-trials,
Pressed to their lips with equal comfort
The dear glove of their lady.
But I sit and chew in vexation
An old herring, my salty comforter,
Midst caterwauling and dogged tribulation.

Meanwhile the ship wrestles
With the wild billowy tide.
Like a rearing war-horse she stands erect,
Upon her stern, till the helm cracks.
Now crashes she headforemost downward once more
Into the howling abyss of waters,
Then again, as if recklessly love-languid,
She tries to recline
On the black bosom of the gigantic waves,
Which powerfully seethe upward,
And immediately a chaotic ocean-cataract

Plunges down in crisp-curling whiteness,
    And covers me with foam.

This shaking and swinging and tossing
        Is unendurable!
Vainly mine eye peers forth and seeks
The German coast. But alas! only water,
And everywhere water, turbulent water!

    Even as the traveller in winter, thirsts
    For a warm cordial cup of tea,
So does my heart now thirst for thee
        My German fatherland.
May thy sweet soil ever be covered
With lunacy, hussars and bad verses,

And thin, lukewarm treatises.
May thy zebras ever be fattened
On roses instead of thistles.
Ever may thy noble apes
Haughtily strut in negligent attire,
And esteem themselves better than all other
Priggish heavy-footed, horned cattle.
May thine assemblies of snails
Ever deem themselves immortal
Because they crawl forward so slowly;
And may they daily convoke in full force,
To discuss whether the cheesemould belongs to the cheese;
And still longer may they convene
To decide how best to honor the Egyptian sheep,
    So that its wool may improve
    And it may be shorn like others,
    With no difference.
    Forever may folly and wrong
    Cover thee all over, oh Germany,

Nevertheless I yearn towards thee
For at least thou art dry land.

X. IN PORT

Happy the man who has reached port,
And left behind the sea and the tempest,
And who now sits, quietly and warm,
In the goodly town-cellar of Bremen.

How pleasantly and cordially
The world is mirrored in the wine-glass.
And how the waving microcosm
Pours sunnily down into the thirsty heart!
I see everything in the glass,
Ancient and modern tribes,
Turks and Greeks, Hegel and Cans,
Citron groves and guard-parades,
Berlin and Schilda, and Tunis and Hamburg.
Above all the image of my beloved,
The little angel-head against the golden background
            of Rhine-wine.

Oh how beautiful! how beautiful thou art, beloved!
        Thou art like a rose.
    Not like the Rose of Shiraz,
The Hafiz-besung bride of the nightingale.
    Not like the Rose of Sharon,
The sacred purple extolled by the prophet.
Thou art like the rose in the wine-cellar of Bremen.
        That is the rose of roses,
    The older it grows the fairer it blooms,
    And its celestial perfume has inspired me.
And did not mine host of the town-cellar of Bremen
        Hold me fast, fast by my hair,
    I should tumble head over heels.

The worthy man! we sat together,
     And drank like brothers.
We spake of lofty, mysterious things,
We sighed and sank in each other's arms.
And he led me back to the religion of love:
I drank to the health of my bitterest enemy,
     And I forgave all bad poets,
As I shall some day hope to be forgiven myself.
I wept with fervor of piety, and at last
The portals of salvation were opened to me,
Where the twelve Apostles, the holy wine-butts,
Preach in silence and yet so intelligibly
     Unto all people.

     Those are men!
Without, unseemly in their wooden garb,
Within, they are more beautiful and brilliant
Than all the haughty Levites of the Temple,
And the guards and courtiers of Herod,
Decked with gold and arrayed in purple.
     But I have always averred
That not amidst quite common folk
     No, in the very best society,
Perpetually abides the King of Heaven.

     Hallelujah! How lovely around me
     Wave the palms of Beth-El!
How fragrant are the myrrh-trees of Hebron!
How the Jordan rustles and reels with joy!
And my immortal soul also reels,
And I reel with her, and, reeling,
The worthy host of the town-cellar of Bremen
Leads me up-stairs into the light of day.

Thou worthy host of the town-cellar of Bremen,
    Seest thou on the roofs of the houses,
Sit the angels, and they are drunk and they sing.
      The glowing sun up yonder
      Is naught but a red drunken nose.
    The nose of the spirit of the universe,
And around the red nose of the spirit of the universe
    Reels the whole tipsy world.

XI. EPILOGUE

Like the stalks of wheat in the fields,
So nourish and wave in the mind of man
      His thoughts.
But the delicate fancies of love
Are like gay little intermingled blossoms
      Of red and blue flowers.

      Red and blue flowers!
The surly reaper rejects you as useless.
The wooden flail scornfully thrashes you,
      Even the luckless traveler,
Whom your aspect delights and refreshes,
      Shakes his head,
And calls you beautiful weeds.

      But the rustic maiden,
      The wearer of garlands,
    Honors you, and plucks you,
And adorns with you her fair locks.
And thus decorated she hastens to the dancing-green
    Where the flutes and fiddles sweetly resound;
      Or to the quiet bushes
Where the voice of her beloved soundeth sweeter still
      Than fiddles or flutes.

Illustrations

Moritz Daniel Oppenheim, Portrait of Heinrich Heine, 1800,
Düsseldorf

Heinrich Heine in 1829

Heinrich Heine in 1837

Heinrich Heine

I

HEINRICH HEINE

Our lyrical poetry is a product of spiritualism, although its material is
sensualistic, the longing of the isolated mind to be merged with the
world of phenomena, to mingle with nature. As sensualism triumphs,
lyrical poetry must end, for there arises a longing for the spiritual:
sentimentality, which grows ever thinner and fainter, nihilistic
mawkishness, a hollow fog of verbiage, a halfway house between
has–been and will–be, tendentious poetry.

Heinrich Heine, epitaph[1]

Christian Johann Heinrich Heine[2] was born in Düsseldorf on
December 13, 1797 and died in Paris on February 17, 1856. Some
of Heine's best-known works were *Briefe aus Berlin, Almansor,
William Ratcliff, Lyrisches Intermezzo, Reisebilder, The North Sea,
Book of Songs, Der Salon, Shakespeares Mädchen und Frauen, New
Poems, Atta Troll: Ein Sommernachtstraum, Der Doktor Faust,* and
Lutezia. Heine's *Leider* were set to music by, among others, Robert
Schumann, Franz Schubert, Felix Mendelssohn, Johannes Brahms,
Richard Strauss, Peter Tchaikovsky, and Richard Wagner.

1 H. Heine, quoted in Michael Hamburger: *Reason and Energy,* 161.
2 The poems in this edition of *The North Sea* are taken from *Poems and Ballads,* tranlsated by
Emma Lazarus (d. 1887), published by R. Worthington, New York, NY, 1881.

Heinrich Heine wrote all manner of poems, from topical and political pieces to meditations of Hebraic culture and Christianity. He created all manner of texts and books, from studies of the Romantic era to lyrical poems.[3] He was one of the late Romantics, and wrote critically and ironically of his Romantic forebears in *Der romantische Schule*.[4] Some of Heine's finest work among his lyrical poetry is his love poetry.[5] Love is a central experience in Romanticism. Friedrich Schlegel, of whom Heine was very critical, wrote that love 'is an intimation of the higher, the infinite, a hieroglyph of the one eternal love, of the sacred, life-abundance of creative nature'.[6] There is not space to discuss his satirical work, his political writings,[7] his relation with British culture,[8] his relation to Jewish culture,[9] and the elements of philosophy and mythology in his poetry.[10]

Like Francesco Petrarch and William Shakespeare, Heinrich Heine was a very self-conscious poet, conscious of the function and poetics of poetry, and its reception by an audience. He was aware of his audience, and cultivated a relationship with his audience, as his Prefaces show, and as comments such as this from the Postscript to *Romancero*: 'An author winds up by getting used to his public as if it were a rational being.'[11]

The North Sea cycle of poems (inspired by Heinrich Heine's visits to Norderney, an East Frisian Island, in 1825-27), presents the archetypal Romantic situation, depicted in a number of different ways but all basically revolving around Romantic subjectivity. Heine creates the typical Poet Alone scenario: the poet at night on a windswept beach. The image has all the ingredients of Romanticism: the sense of the infinite in the spaces

---

3 See Jeffrey L. Samons, 1979 and 1969; S.S. Pawer, 1961; Barker Fairley, 1963; A.I. Sandor, 1967.
4 H. Heine: *Der romantische Schule*, 1971.
5 See S.S. Pawer, 1960.
6 Friedrich Schlegel, II, 334.
7 See William Ross, 1956; Nigel Reeves, 1974.
8 See S.S. Pawer, 1986.
9 See S.S. Pawer, 1983; Israel Tabak, 1948.
10 See Robert C. Holub, 1981.
11 H. Heine: *Complete Poems*, 696.

of sea; light and dark (stars shining amidst black night); feminine mysteries (night itself, the fecund ocean, etc); solitude and subjectivity; the aristocratic ego against the world; desire, which comes from the space around the poet, the distance between him and what he desires, the vast space indicating his separateness from other people, in particular the beloved woman; nature – lots of nature in that sea and sky's motion – the sea *never* stops moving; ecstasy – the poet feeling ecstatic being alone beside the ocean; mysticism – being alone amidst nature allows the poet to muse upon pantheism and the One and All; religious unity – the poet sees the Oversoul or World-Soul in all things, sees all things as one, and himself at the centre of everything. All these things are expressed in Heine's poet alone on the beach beside the North Sea: this is all of the poem 'Declaration':

All dusked in shadow came the evening,
Wilder tumbled the waves,
And I sat on the shores and gazed at
The white dance of the billows,
And my heart swelled up like the sea,
And a longing seized me, deep homesickness
For you, the lovely image
That everywhere haunts me
And everywhere calls to me,
Everywhere, everywhere,
In the howl of the wind, in the growl of the sea,
And in the sighing of my own breast.
With slender reed I wrote on the sand,
"Agnes, I love you!"
But cruel waves washed in
Over the sweet confession
And blotted it out.

You fragile reed, you crumbling sand,
You fugitive waves, I trust you no more!
The heavens grow darker, my heart grows wilder,
And with mighty hand, from Norway's forests
I wrench the tallest fir tree
And dip it deep
Into Etna's burning maw, and with this

Fiery-tipped pen of giants
I write on the darkling dome of heaven,
"Agnes, I love you!"

Every night since then they burn
Up there, the eternal words of flame,
And all the children of men to come
Will joy to read the heavenly words:
"Agnes, I love you!" (137)

The poet alone on the windy strand feels ecstasy but still feels a lack, and a desire. There is still the beloved woman, in his past and perhaps in his future, which he has not conquered. We see Heinrich Heine's poet here making a massive gesture, painting his love in fire on the heavens, verily an act of Promethean-like proportions. It is an out-size performance, bigger than art, a mythic act.

No, the poet, no matter how self-contained he may be in his subjectivity, still yearns for the beloved woman. So, when he looks at the stars, he sees her eyes, he gasps:

They're her eyes, the stars up yonder,
My love's eyes
(in 'A Night in the Cabin', 138)

Heinrich Heine simultaneously mocks this yearning, Romantic tradition even as he exalts it. Restlessness is his hallmark as a poet, in one sense, as it is of poets such as Arthur Rimbaud and Percy Bysshe Shelley. More interesting is when Heine moves off the subject of love, and thrills to the splendours of nature. He can be an extraordinary nature poet, as mystical and powerful as the best of them (William Wordsworth, Johann Wolfgang von Goethe, Emily Dickinson). In 'Ship-wrecked', Heine conjures up the notion of a 'black sun' (central to D.H. Lawrence's mythopœia):

O my jet-black sun how often –
How thrilling-often I drank from you
Wild flames of inspiration,

And stood and reeled, as if drunk with fire,
And then a dove-mild smile came hovering
About your proud full-curving lips
And your proud full-curving lips
Breathed out words as sweet as moonlight
And tender as roses' fragrance –
And my soul was lifted up
And soared like an eagle up to the heavens! (148)

Heinrich Heine is well aware of the pitfalls of being so rapturous in poetry, and much of his rapture is in fact irony. For Karl Kraus, Heine's poetry was imitation, a synthetic Romanticism.[12] The problem is the distinctions between irony and straight-faced poetry are not always made clear, and an ambivalence abounds in his work. His attitude to women, for instance, are fraught with loathing as well as love. In Heine's poetry, as in the art of Goethe, Novalis, Friedrich Hölderlin, Michael Drayton, Alfred de Musset and any male poet you care to mention, there is an ambiguous attitude towards women and things 'feminine'. Fear and desire are the twin poles of Heine's work, as of so many poets' work. So that, finally, fear and desire express themselves in an ironic mode, which knows full well how art digs its own grave. Or as Heine puts it in a short lyric:

Day and night I've poetized,
Yet gained nothing that I prized;
Though my harmony's unsurpassed,
This has got me nowhere fast. (277)

Francesco Petrarch and William Shakespeare too knew well how the very act of writing complicates and adds to the problem it is trying to grapple with. Thus, writing about love is therapy on one level. It deals with feelings of loss and yearning. On another level, though, writing of love simply exaggerates the fact that one is *not in love*, or with the beloved right at that moment. For, if one were in love (or lying beside the beloved), one would not be writing about love. Henri Matisse spoke of painting in the same

---

12 Karl Kraus: *Mein Gutachten*, in *Literature and Lüge*, Munich 1962, 39-41.

way: 'I too have said one wouldn't paint if one were happy. I'm in agreement with Picasso on that one. We have to live over a volcano.'[13] If one was really happy, one would not write poetry. Art, it seems, comes out of dissatisfaction, an ontological restlessness. We see this so clearly in the Romantics, in Percy Bysshe Shelley or Heinrich Heine, John Keats or Friedrich Schlegel. J. P. Stern writes in *The Heart of Europe*::

> If there is one theme which German poets of the last three centuries have made peculiarly and poignantly their own, it is their concern with the world as a place of insecurity and impermanence, a provisional state...[14]

Heinrich Heine thrives on restlessness, on argument, on Hegelian dialectical discourse. For instance, he writes in the *Romancero* Postscript: 'Yes, I have returned to God, like the prodigal son, after a long time of tending swine with the Hegelians.' (695)

It is not simply a question of a dualism of ethics where spirituality is on one side and sensuality on the other, for, as Michael Hamburger notes, '"sensualism" too was a religion' (*Reason*, 149). Heinrich Heine's cult of sensuality contains contradictions, not least with Judæo-Christianity, which constituted the 'religion of pain' as Heine termed it. Like Oswald Spengler in *The Decline of the West*, Heine regarded the Christian era as a disease, a falling away, a decay of world culture after the ecstasy and refinement of ancient Greece. Or as he put it in *Memoirs of Herr von Schnabelewopski*: 'Our age – and it begins at the Cross of Christ – will be regarded as a great period of human illness.'[15]

Heinrich Heine seems to be accurate here, but this was by no means Heine's fixed view. His views often changed. Sensuality, in Heine's view, becomes a part of a pantheistic Christianity, if it is not already too contradictory to put pantheism and Christianity together. Indeed, William Wordsworth and the English Romantics

13 H. Matisse, quoted in Pierre Schneider: Matisse, Rizzoli, New York 1984, 734.
14 J. Stern: *The Heart of Europe: Essays on Literature and Ideology*, Blackwell 1992, 307.
15 H. Heine: *Works*, 1, 545.

readily fused Christianity and pantheism, speaking on the one hand of the Christian Father-God, and on the other hand of the 'One and All', the 'world-soul' or Oversoul that pervades everything, that is and is not the Judæo-Christian God. Heine wrote:

> Sounds and words, colours and shapes, sensuous phenomena of every kind are only symbols of an idea, symbols that arise in the artist's mind when it is moved by the holy World Spirit; his works of art are only symbols by which he communicates his own ideas to other minds.[16]

One can take all of Heinrich Heine's poetry as parody and irony, but then, not many writers create hundreds of pages of mockery without also having something of the attitude of the 'erotic irony' that Thomas Mann spoke about, where the mocker actually loves what is being mocked (otherwise, what would be the point? Why waste so much time writing so much poetry if one hates everything about one's subject?). In Heine's love poetry, despite the parodies and imitations, there is an undercurrent of desire that seems to be authentic. A yearning that parody cannot erase. There is, under the sarcasm and bile, gentle thoughts at times, an idealism in Heine's poetry, even a utopianism, which surfaces from time to time, as in this famous extract from his *History*:

> Happier and more beautiful generations, conceived in rarely chosen embraces, who grow up in a religion of joy, will smile sorrowfully at their poor ancestors, who gloomily abstained from all the pleasures of this fair earth, and, by deadening their warm and colourful senses, were reduced almost to chilly spectres. Yes, I saw it with certainty, our descendants will be happier and more beautiful than we. For I believe in progress, I believe that mankind is destined to be happy, and thus I think more highly of divinity than those pious people who think mankind was created only to suffer. Here on earth, by the blessings of free political and industrial institutions, I should like to establish that bliss which, in the opinion of the pious, will come only in heaven, on the day of judgment.[17]

---

16 Quoted in M. Hamburger: *Reason*, 156.
17 H. Heine: *Works*, 3, 518-9.

Heinrich Heine's work displays many ambiguities; there is an ambivalence at the heart of his poetry, as he simultaneously explores and sends up poetic methods and ideas. He is a poet who shifts his goals continually, who does not remain fixed in one poetic stance. His early poetry, like that of so many young poets, is full of fervour, emotion and idealism. It is mainly love poetry, this early work, as with Dante Alighieri or William Shakespeare.

Heinrich Heine sings breathlessly of love, of love won and lost, of love, above all, *desired*, so that desire itself is really Heine's subject. Heine is in love with love, not really with the beloved. Love poetry becomes for him, as for Francesco Petrarch and the Italian *stilnovisti*, an elegant mirror that reflects back, as in the myth of Narcissus, his own desire. Poetry is a narcissistic mirror, in which the poet sees his love reflected. His love obscures the beloved woman; she is a springboard, merely, for his artistic excesses. 'To the lover she is the ultimate reality', writes Novalis in his philosophical fragments.[18] We see this so clearly in Dante Alighieri's *Vita Nuova*, where Beatrice Portinari is simply a pretext for poetry, or with Francesco Petrarch and his Laura de Noyes. In Petrarch's *Rime Sparse*, the true 'subject' of the poetry is not Laura but Petrarch himself, the creation of a poem, endlessly polished, honed, shaped, sculpted, cultivated, refined. The troubadour Giraut de Borneil spoke of polishing one's songs (*cansos*) so they would shine, reflecting back his love.

Heinrich Heine's poetry is fiercely heterosexual, as is Francesco Petrarch's or Thomas Hardy's or Edmund Spenser's (Bill Shakespeare, John Donne and Percy Shelley, though, consciously explored the boundaries of gender). Heine loves women, like Robert Graves or Bernard de Ventadour. 'A woman's body is a song', he wrote in 'The Song of Songs',

> God writes it with His Word
> In nature's grandest album when
> His spirit once was stirred. (743)

---

18 Novalis: *Pollen and Fragments*, 60.

Heinrich Heine's early poetry, in the *Book of Songs*, is a mass of seething, youthful, inspired emotions, where the feminine is deeply desired – the erotic as well as spiritual feminine, the woman who is both spirit (there many fairies and apparitions in Heine, as in John Keats's poetry), and erotic and sensual:

In sweetest dream, in silent night,
She came to me with magic's might,
With magic might, my love-in-bloom,
She came to me, to my own room. (14)

This is from 'Dream Pictures', in *Youthful Sorrows*. The age old scenario of a young man erotically conjuring up visions of female sprites at night occurs throughout Heinrich Heine's early poetry. His mythology of love poetry is archetypal Western erotic art, where the woman, as in the poetry of Maurice Scève and Torquato Tasso, is the Jungian *anima* or feminine soul-image, dressed in white ('the maid was white', Heine writes, 12). The archetypal three colours of poetry occur here, the colours of alchemy and magic: black, white and red. Black is the night, the poet's unconscious, 'Mother Night', the all-encompassing world-space or World-Soul out of which the female spirit comes, dressed in white, her face radiant, her eyes shining, her very illumination pierces the poet, and, out of this combination of black and white comes red, the red of blood throbbing and pulsing in sexual arousal ('My blood is wild', Heine writes, 130), the red of passion ('In burning words my passing lows', 15), heat, burning fever and religious intoxication. These three colours, and variations of them, occur throughout love poetry (in Beatrice's red dress in Dante Alighieri's dream in the *Vita Nuova*, for instance, in the colour of countless blushing cheeks in the works of the troubadours, *Minnesängers*, minstrels and *stilnovisti*).

She, the beloved, the desired woman, the Goddess, is a spectre, a phantom, a ghost, a demon. The poet does not realize he has wished her up, like a magician. Magic flows throughout Heinrich Heine's early verse, as it does in William Shakespeare (*A*

Midsummer Night's Dream and *Love's Labour's Lost*, for instance).
Magic is that stuff that enables the spirit-woman to appear, that
allows the poet to speak of such things, that encourages the
shamanic night journeys of the dreaming artist/ autist. Dreaming
is central to Heine's poetry:

> When I lie on my pallet,
> Embraced by night, I trace
> Hovering there before me
> An image of sweet grace. (96)

Heinrich Heine, like so many poets before and after him,
acknowledged the notion of the poet as shaman, the poet as wish-
fulfilling magician. Indeed, Heine identified with Merlin the
magician, as William Shakespeare's Prospero did (with more than
a hint of John Dee thrown in, in Prospero's case). In the Postscript
to *Romancero*, when he was bed-ridden – he called the bed his
'mattress-grave' – Heine identified with Merlin being emprisoned
late in his life:

> My body has shrivelled so much that almost nothing is left but the
> voice, and my bed reminds me of the tolling grave of the magician
> Merlin, which lies in the forest of Brozeliand in Brittany, under tall
> oaks whose tops shoot up to heaven like green flames. Ah, I envy you,
> dear colleague Merlin, these trees and the fresh breezes blowing
> through them, for there is not a single green leaf rustling here in my
> mattress-grave in Paris. (693)

Merlin the magician was, legend has it, imprisoned by the
enchantress Nimue. Merlin was
a slave, ultimately, of the feminine power and mysteries, as
was Prospero, who got all his magical powers from the Witch
Sycorax. Prospero lived in the domain of the Eternal Feminine, as
did Faust and Merlin. They drew on the Goddess for their
powers. Heinrich Heine, too, can be seen as a Goddess-orientated
poet, a 'Muse-poet', to use Robert Graves' terminology, a poet
who lived in the thrall of his Muse, a woman both real and

spiritual, both erotic and æthereal. In 'Katharina', Heine wrote:

> Like sage Merlin, I am bound
> By the magic spell I wrought;
> In the end I'm snared and caught
> On my own enchanted ground. (358)

Maurice Scève was enslaved by Délie, and Sir Philip Sidney's Astrophel with Stella, and William Shakespeare with the fair youth, and Edmund Spenser with Gloriana, and so on.

Heinrich Heine's early poetry, especially in his *Book of Songs*, can be seen as Goddess poetry. In the Preface to the second edition, Heine wrote:

> ...first of all come songs which were written in those earlier years when the first kisses of the German muse were burning in my soul. Ah, the kisses of that excellent wench have since lost much of their ardor and freshness! Under such long-standing conditions the fervency of the honeymoon is bound to cool down gradually, but tenderness often becomes so much the more deeply felt, especially on bad days, and thus it was the German muse showed me all of her love and fidelity! (4-5)

You can find the Muse or the Goddess in most places in Heinrich Heine's poetry, not just in the *Book of Songs*. There are many poems to particular women, for instance: Seraphine, Psyche, the Unknown She, Katharina, Friedrike, Emma, Clarisse, Hortense, Diana, Angelique, real and mythical women, written in the middle period.

In the *Lyrical Intermezzo*, Heinrich Heine wrote of the archetypal dream-woman:

> Then in glides his loved one, in shimmering clothes
> Of sea foam mantling her graces;
> She flows and glows like a blossoming rose,
> Her veil is of jewelled laces.
> Her golden hair flutters around her pale form,
> Her sweet eyes invite him, passionate, warm –
> They fall in each other's embraces. (51)

The dream-woman here is an archetypal erotic object, at once sensual and spiritual, anchored by allusions to roses, one of *the* symbols prime of the Eternal Feminine, a symbol which combines love and death in multi-faceted ways. Other usual trappings of spiritual-women are here: the images of light (golden hair, shimmering clothes), the seductive eyes, images of heat (the warm embrace), the flowing, sensuous movements, the allusions to the appearance of Venus rising from the sea (sea foam), and the veil. Veils have to be pierced or drawn aside by the errant knight, who is the questing, phallic male; he has to move beyond each layer to get to the heart of the woman, her spiritual and emotional centre, which is her vulva (symbolized in so many poets by the rose).

Like much Romantic poetry, Heinrich Heine's is very erotic – not simply sensual, but deeply erotic. As when he writes of the beloved's mouth:

> Her red mouth, rich and velvety
> Gave me a kiss that set my lips aglow (49)

Thomas Hardy wrote similarly erotically of Tess's mouth in *Tess of the d'Urbervilles*. Or when Heine links love and pain in the kiss of a lover (recalling the *mors osculis*, the kiss of death of occultism):

> You hurt my lips with kisses, so
> Now kiss the pain away (174)

For Heinrich Heine, lying in the embrace of a lover's arms is the way to heaven, as with the troubadours and *Minnesängers* (an early poem in *Book of Songs* was entitled 'The Minnesingers'). The troubadours might prefer to say 'lying between a woman's legs' rather than, in the Romantic, more fastidious fashion, 'in a lover's embrace'. For Heine, spiritual and sexual ecstasy fuse, and the lover's embrace enables religious rapture:

> When she embraced me, tenderly clinging,

My soul flew heavenward, flew straight up! (174)

Or again, lyrics from *Lyrical Intermezzo:*

Beloved woman, embrace me
With love encompassing;
Let your arms and legs enlace me,
Your supple body cling. (171)

It's all there in Heinrich Heine's poetry, the merging of the sensual and the spiritual, where the flesh-and-blood beloved merges into various incarnations of the spiritual or fairy woman. In the art of Dante Alighieri and Francesco Petrarch, Beatrice and Laura merge into the Virgin Mary, as also in John Donne and Edmund Spenser. In Heine's poetry, the beloved is compared to an angel, a fairy, a spirit, and so on. In *Lyrical Intermezzo*, she is compared to that holy of holies in Arthurian romance, the Holy Grail (53), which as Jungians remind us, is a fount or cauldron of feminine mysteries, a world-womb out of which flows life itself.

And so Heinrich Heine goes on to draw together heaps of mediæval imagery, floral symbolism (eyes like violets), Christian mysticism (embodied by cathedrals, the Virgin Mary), Classical mythology ('foam born child of ocean', 57), and *stilnovisti* conceits (sweet eyes, sweet lips, sweet cheeks, eyes like flowers, cheeks of red roses, hands like white lilies, 61).

Heinrich Heine's *Book of Songs* is essentially a story of desire, desire felt and thwarted, as in Johann Wolfgang von Goethe's *Faust* or *Young Werther,* or Novalis' *Hymns To the Night.* Desire suffuses most of Heine's poetry, as it does with William Shakespeare's plays or D.H. Lawrence's novels. The *Book of Songs* depicts many scenes of weeping, pathetic tears and claspings, partings, or sitting alone on the beach, at sunset ('We sat in the lonely fisher's shack,/ We sat there silent, alone', he writes in *The Homecoming,* 82). A recurring theme in Heine's output is the vision of female visitors to the dreaming man by night, the sprites who appear in erotic embraces with the sleeping knight, as in

'Dream and Life' from *Youthful Sorrows*, where fairies dance around him (169).

II

THE GERMAN ROMANTIC WORLD

The world must be romanticized.

Novalis, *Pollen and Fragments* (56)

Just as poetry is the most original, the arche-and mother-art of all the others, poetry will also be the ultimate perfection of humanity, the ocean into which however far it may have moved away from it in various forms.

A.W. Schlegel[19]

This chapter looks at German Romantic poetry chiefly in terms of its poetic, lyrical, magical, spiritual and erotic aspects. That is, poetry as poetry. The world of German Romantic poetry holds many of the same tenets as that of British or French Romanticism. We are not concerned here with definitions of the term 'Romanticism', which are discussed by critics elsewhere. Our definition of the term 'Romanticism' is of a lyrical, emotional, religious and self-conscious form of art which can be applied to many modern artists, as well as the Romantics themselves.

---

19 A.W. Schlegel, 1989-, I, 388.

'Romanticism' is used loosely, though applied mainly to the artists of the Romantic era, the late 18th and early 19th centuries. One can just as easily read Johann Wolfgang von Goethe, for instance, as a 'Classical' artist. Ditto Friedrich Schlegel, Novalis or Friedrich Hölderlin.[20] We are here studying the work of the poets, but not so much whether they were 'Classic' or 'Romantic', though connections will be made, from time to time, between Romanticism and modernism.[21]

The hallmarks of poetic Romanticism include the following:

Infinity.
'A work is shaped when it is everywhere sharply delimited, but within those limits limitless and inexhaustible; when it is completely faithful to itself, homogeneous, and nonetheless exalted above itself', wrote Karl Wilhelm Friedrich Schlegel in the *Athenaeum*.[22] The German Romantic poets, like the British and French writers, stretch themselves to infinity. If 'infinity' is an 'impossible' concept, scientifically, that does not bother the Romantics. They yearn towards infinity – in all things. As Percy Bysshe Shelley wrote in *A Defence of Poetry*, '[a] poet participates in the eternal, the infinite, and the one'.[23] Romanticism sometimes gives other names to its infinity-drive or extremism: the 'absolute' for instance, is frequently used: Romantics speak of absolute unity, absolute feeling, absolute art.

This extremism is a key component of Romanticism, whether it is the Romanticism of Johann Wolfgang von Goethe, Percy Shelley, Alfred de Musset or Novalis. Later artists, too, spoke of the necessity of 'going to extremes', such as André Gide, who

---

20 In German Romanticism, everyone is called 'Friedrich', or 'Wilhelm'.
21 See Jürgen Habermas: *The Philosophical Discourse of Modernity*, tr. Frederick Lawrence, MIT Press, Cambridge Mass., 1987. On German Romanticism, see David Simpson *et al*, eds: *German Aesthetic and Literary Criticism*, Cambridge University Press, 3 vols, 1984-5; H.G. Schenk: *The Mind of the European Romantics*, Constable 1966; M.H. Abrams, 1971; Manfred Brown, 1979; Philippe Lacoue-Labarthe, 1988; Azade Seyhan: *Representation and its Discontents: The Critical Legacy of German Romanticism*, University of California Press, Berkeley 1992.
22 F. Schlegel: *Lucinde and the Fragments*, 297.
23 P. Shelley: *Selected Poetry and Prose*, ed. Alisdair D.F. Macrae, Routledge 1991, 207.

wrote of extremism in his 1890s fiction, *Paludes*. Any number of post-Romantic artists use the doctrine of extremism or going to infinity: William Burroughs with his outrageously violent novels, D.H. Lawrence with his wild flights of polemic, the painter Mark Rothko's canvases, everywhere regarded as 'Romantic', or Friedrich Nietzsche's philosophy.

Feeling.

Deep emotions, feelings or sensibilities are one of the most obvious marks of Romanticism. Romantic poetry goes mad with emotion, passion, elation. Romantic poetry can be reduced to one word: *desire*. It is all about desire, about the gulf between desire and satisfaction, between present desire and past fulfilment. As Heinrich Heine writes in *The Homecoming*:

> They both were in love, but neither
> To the other ever confessed;
> They acted so very unfriendly,
> And love burned high in each breast.[24]

Romantic poetry pivots around the Lacanian *lack*; the creation of Romantic poetry, as of nearly all poetry except that written to order, stems from some kind of desire. In Romantic poetry, the desire is for all manner of things – for love, connection, nature, infinity, ecstasy, etc. A.W. Schlegel speaks of the Romantic poetry of desire:

> The poetry of the ancients was the poetry of possession, our poetry is that of yearning; the former stands firmly on the ground of the present, the latter sways between memory and presentiment.[25]

Romantic poetry is fraught with all manner of tensions. One of the most fundamental is that between sacred and secular love. Love must be spiritualized, made transcendent, the Romantic poets contend. Or, as Friedrich Schlegel says, sacred and profane

---

24 H. Heine: *Complete Poems*, 90.
25 A.W. Schlegel: *Sämtliche Werke*, ed. Eduard Böcking, Weidmann, Leipzig 1846, 5.

love must be harmonized. This form of spiritual love is, Schlegel writes: 'an intimation of the higher, the infinite, a hieroglyph of the one eternal love, of the sacred life-abundance of creative nature.'[26]

Ecstasy.

The apotheosis of feeling or desire in (German) Romantic poetry is ecstasy, just as in traditional religion. Ecstasy comes from all manner of input, ranging from nature contemplation through love and sex to drugs (the opiates, morphine or laudanum or whatever). Ecstasy is a goal of some (not all) Romantic poets. Novalis, John Keats and Friedrich Hölderlin were shamanic poets who at times whipped up storms of rapture. The sensual nature of Romantic poetry is obvious. At times, Romantic poetry is orgasmic, and the lush imagery, floods of words and shamanic energy combine to create an bliss of poetry, an erotic lyricism that is certainly one of the main reasons why Romantic poetry continues to be so enjoyed by readers, and exalted by critics.

The Romantic poets burst life back into poetry, and their poetic personas (quite distinct from the poets as flesh and blood people, the subjects of biographies), burst into life themselves. So much of Romantic poetry is full of rapture, expressed in those single words – *life, love, soul, world* – energized by being written with capitals, accompanied by exclamation marks, so they become 'Life! Love! Soul! World!' Percy Bysshe Shelley's exuberant outburst is probably the most famous example of rapturous, exclamation marks Romanticism:

I

O world! O life! O time!
On whose last steps I climb,
   Trembling at that where I had stood before;
When will return the glory of your prime?
         No more – Oh, nevermore!

---

26 F. Schlegel, 1958-, II, 334.

II

Out of the day and night
A joy has taken flight;
   Fresh spring, and summer, and winter hoar,
Move my faint heart with grief, but with delight
      No more – Oh, never more!

Mysticism.

Romantic poetry, and especially German Romantic poetry, is mystical. It is a religion on its own. It is a mystical cult, with its own initiations, rituals, beliefs, heresies and ecstasies. Friedrich Schlegel spoke of German Romantic poetry as something of a religion. Novalis and Schlegel referred to their attempt at founding a new religion.[27] Heinrich Heine was more criticial of world religions than some of his contemporaries.

Novalis is the most obviously, flamboyantly mystical of the German Romantic poets, but Friedrich Hölderlin, Johann Wolfgang von Goethe and Heinrich Heine are no less mystical. That is, Novalis is unabashed about his mysticality: he leaps in, wholeheartedly.

Friedrich Hölderlin's poetry, especially his early lyrics, is powerfully shamanic; it is full of shamanic imagery, as is the early poetry of Percy Shelley or Francesco Petrarch. In Hölderlin's poetry we find images of light, of bliss, of motion, of revelation, all shamanic/ religious motifs. Heinrich Heine's view of the poet as shaman was more political, aware of the role of the poet in societal revolutions:

Our age is warmed by the idea of human equality, and the poets, who as high priests do homage to this divine sun, can be certain that thousands kneel down beside them, and that thousands weep and rejoice with them.[28]

---

27 See Ernst Behler, 158.
28 H. Heine: *The Works of Heinrich Heine*, 432.

Greece.

Romantic poets exalt Greek culture – Friedrich Hölderlin with his Hellenic hymns, for instance. A.W. Schlegel wrote that Greek culture was 'a perfect natural education', that Greek religion was the 'worship of natural forces and of earthly life', that the Greek concept of beauty was 'a purified, ennobled sensuality', that Greek art was a 'poetics of joy', the 'expression of the consciousness of this harmony of all forces'.[29]

All of the major German Romantic poets look back to Greece and, especially, to Greek mythology (but also back to the mediæval era, to the Renaissance, to poets such as William Shakespeare, Dante Alighieri and Giovanni Boccaccio, to the Orient, and to the early years of Christianity. The Schlegels studied Dante, Shakespeare, Boccaccio, Miguel de Cervantes, Francesco Petrarch, Calderón, Portuguese and Provençal poets).[30]

For the Romantics, the pantheon of Greek Gods and Goddesses were not simply reduced to words but fully alive beings, each with their own history, identity, personality and relationships.

Mythology/ Folklore.

A.W. Schlegel wrote: 'Myth, like language, general, a necessary product of the human poetic power, an arche-poetry of humanity'.[31] Much of German Romanticism uses all kinds of folklore – the Grimms, for instance, with their very influential collection and rewriting of fairy tales; Ludwig von Tieck's works contain much fantastic material, and he uses fairy tales in his fictions, including Charles Perrault's *Puss in Boots* fairy tale in his *Der gestiefelte Kater*;[32] Novalis wrote of fairy tales: 'All fairy tales are dreams of that homelike world that is everywhere and

---

29 A.W. Schlegel: *Sämtliche Werke*, op.cit., 5, 12-3.
30 See F. Schlegel, 1958, III, 17-37; E. Behler, 154; A.W. Schlegel: *Spanisches Theater*, Reimer, Berlin 1803-9, I, 2, 72-87.
31 A.W. Schlegel, 1989-, I, 49.
32 See Rolf Stamm: *Ludwig Tieck's späte Novellen*, Kohlhamer, Stuttgart 1973; Raimund Belgardt: "Poetic Imagination and External Reality in Tieck", *Essays in German Literature Festschrift*, ed. Michael S. Batts, University of British Columbia Press, 1968, 41-61; Rosemarie Helge: *Motive und Motivstrukturen bei Ludwig Tieck*, Kümmerle, Göppingen 1974.

nowhere.'[33] Many poets looked back to Arthurian legends (John Keats in 'La Belle Dame Sans Merci', for instance); figures such as Isolde and Tristan, Tannhäuser, etc, appear in German Romantic poetry. Romanticism also employs all manner of 'hermetic' or 'occult' thought, from Gnosticism (in Novalis), Qabbalism, Rosicrucianism, alchemy, magic, astronomy, etc (in Franz Brentano's *Die Romanzen vom Rosenkrantz*, alchemy in Johann Wolfgang von Goethe's *Faust*, etc).

Paganism.

The Hellenism ties in (and is inextricable from) the paganism of Romanticism. The German Romantics, like their British counter-parts, exalted pagan beliefs, though theirs was a stylized, self-conscious form of paganism, which took up certain beliefs or rites and ignored others. Heinrich Heine wrote that the first Romantics

> acted out of a pantheistic impulse of which they themselves were not aware. The feeling which they believed to be a nostalgia for the Catholic Mother Church was of deeper origin than they guessed, and their reverence and preference for the heritage of the Middle Ages, for the popular beliefs, diabolism, magical practices, and witchcraft of that era... all this was a suddenly reawakened but unrecognized leaning toward the pantheism of the ancient Germans.[34]

The paganism of Romanticism is a part of pantheism, as in the Classicism of painters such as Nicolas Poussin and Claude Lorrain, or nature worship. Heinrich Heine called pantheism 'the secret religion of Germany'.[35]

Nature.

The Romantics exalted nature (German Romanticism had its 'Naturphilosophie', a non-scientific notion stemming partly from Friedrich Wilhelm Joseph Schelling and Georg Wilhelm Friedrich Hegel). But, again, nature is mediated through the highly self-conscious and heavily stylized mechanisms of poetry. Images of

33 Novalis: *Novalis Schriften*, 2, 564.
34 H. Heine: *Salon II*, 1852, 250-1.
35 H. Heine: *Works*, 3, 571.

nature abound in most forms of Romantic poetry. Nature is the backdrop to their poetic out-pourings, but it is always nature seen from the vantage point of culture.

In *The Sorrows of Young Werther*, Johann Wolfgang von Goethe speaks of 'my heart's immense and ardent feeling for living Nature, which overwhelmed me with so great a joy and made the world about me a very paradise'. He goes on to evoke rivers and hilltops right out of European landscape painting, and 'lovely clouds which a soft evening breeze wafted across the heavens'.

> I felt as if I had been made a god in that overwhelming abundance, and the glorious forms of infinite Creation moved in my soul, giving it life. Immense mountains surrounded me, chasms yawned at my feet, streams swollen by rain tumbled headlong, rivers flowed below me and the forests and mountains resounded. (65)

Heinrich Heine has written, like so many other poets, of the eroticism of Spring – 'the magic month of May', Heine writes.[36] 'Testament' ('Vermächt') of 1829 speaks breathlessly of philosophical idealism, where nothing is lost, for 'all' lives in the 'All':

> No thing on earth to nought can fall,
> The Eternal onward moves in all;
> Rejoice, by being be sustained.
> Being is deathless: living wealth,
> With which the all adorns itself,
> By laws abides and is maintained. (267)

There is much darkness in German Romantic (and most Romantic) poetry: big, windy moonlit skies such as, in later literature, fill Tom Brangwen's head in *The Rainbow* by D.H. Lawrence, or Arthur Rimbaud's soul in *A Season in Hell*, or, most obviously, that blow right through the work of Rainer Maria Rilke, ending up as the shamanic forces of the Angel in the *Duino Elegies*. These huge, cloudy, rainy, windy spaces are to be found not only in Johann Wolfgang von Goethe's poetry and his *Faust*,

36 H. Heine: *Complete Poems*, 52.

but also in Joseph Freiherr von Eichendorff's lyrics, in, of course, Novalis' *Hymnen an die Nacht*, or in Heinrich Heine's *The North Sea* cycle, where the poet languishes on a nocturnal strand straight out of a Caspar David Friedrich painting.

Idealism.

German Romantic poetry, like all Romantic poetry (like all poetry, one might say), has idealistic and utopian elements. German Romantic poetry, in particular, is marked by a vivacious, sometimes ridiculous idealism, which comes as much from Plato as from Immanuel Kant. 'Transcendental idealism' is a term often applied to German Romantic poetics. 'I call transcendental all knowledge which is not so much occupied with objects as with the mode of our cognition of objects', wrote Immanuel Kant in the *Critique of Pure Reason*,[37] underlining the subjectivity (as with René Descartes) that is at the centre of post-Renaissance philosophy. There is a philosophy, Johann Gottlieb Fichte argued, that is beyond being and beyond consciousness, a philosophy that aims for 'the absolute unity between their separateness.'[38]

Unity.

'The new mythology must be forged from the deepest depths of the spirit; it must be the most artful of all works of art, for it must encompass all others; a new bed and vessel for the ancient, eternal fountainhead of poetry', wrote Friedrich Schlegel.[39] One of the key elements of Romantic poetry, of German Romantic poetry especially, and of all poetry generally, is the concept of unity. For the poet, all things are connected together.

> In our mind [wrote Novalis], everything is connected in the most peculiar, pleasant, and lively manner. The strangest things come together by virtue of one space, one time, an odd similarity, an error, some accident. In this manner, curious unities and peculiar connections

37 Immanuel Kant: *Werke*, de Gruyter, Berlin, 1968, III, 43.
38 J. Fichte, letter, 23 June 1804, quoted in E. Behler, 19.
39 F. Schlegel: *Dialogue on Poetry and Literary Aphorisms*, tr. Ernst Behler & Roman Struc, Pennsylvania State University Press, University Park 1968, 81-2.

originate – one thing reminds us of everything, becomes the sign of many things. Reason and imagination are united through time and space in the most extraordinary manner, and we can say that each thought, each phenomenon of our mind is the most individual part of an altogether individual totality.[40]

What connects it all is the poet's sensibility, awareness, imagination, talents, feelings, call them what you will. Poetry is very much like Western magic in this respect. Magicians speak of the cardinal rule of hermeticism and magicke as being the hermetic tenet of the Emerald Table of Hermes Trismegistus: *as above, so below.* This dictum applies to poetry as much to magic. Basically, the view is that all things are one even as they are separate/ different/ scattered everywhere. Sufi mystics speak of 'unity in multiplicity' and 'multiplicity in unity', the 'unity' for them being Allah. For poets and magicians, founded in the Western Neoplatonic, Renaissance, humanist, magical tradition, 'the One' is only occasionally identified with God.

For (the Romantic) poets, the *as above, so below* philosophy means that inner and outer are identical, that what happens inside, psychologically, is mirrored and influences the outer, physical world. The two worlds interconnect and influence each other. As Novalis writes: 'What is outside me, is really within me, is mind – and vice versa'.[41] Further, the world is a continuum for the poet, so that colours are associated with particular planets, say, or angels, or flowers, or metals. This view of the oneness of all things occurs not only in Romantic poetry, but in most of poetry, from Sappho onwards. It is, partly, the basis for the 'pathetic fallacy', the ubiquitous poetic metaphor, where Sappho can say that erotic desire is like a wind shaking oak trees on a mountain-side.

The Romantic philosophy of unity develops into Charles Baud-elaire's 'theory of correspondences', which was later taken up by Arthur Rimbaud, Stéphane Mallarmé and Paul Valéry. Friedrich Schlegel, one of the major theorists of Romantic poetry, speaks of

40 Novalis: *Novalis Schriften*, 3, 650-1.
41 Novalis: *Novalis Schriften*, 3, 429.

Romantic poetry as unifying poetry and philosophy, which is one of the hallmarks of Romantic poetry, German or otherwise. 'Romantic poetry is a progressive universal poetry', wrote Schlegel.[42] He argued for a new mythology of poetry, a universal mythopœia, which would connect all things together, a 'hieroglyphic expression of nature around us'.[43]

Ego / Subjectivity.

Since the Renaissance, 'the One' has been variously interpreted: a common interpretation is that all things relate, ultimately, to the human individual. Renaissance philosophy centres around the individual, where 'man is the measure of all things', embodied in Leonardo da Vinci's famous drawing *The Proportions of the Human Body*.[44] In the Renaissance view, man is at the centre of the universe. This is also very much the Romantic view. Catherine Belsey writes in *Critical Practice*:

> One of the main thrusts of Romanticism is the rejection of an alien world of industrial capitalism, recurrently signified in images of death, disease and decay. Poetry claims to create a living world, fostered by nature but springing essentially from the subjectivity of the poet, from what Coleridge calls the Imagination, a mode of perception which endows the phenomenal world with a vitality and an intensity issuing ultimately from the soul itself... The Romantic rejection of the 'real conditions' is based on a belief in the autonomy of the subject. The 'man possessed of more than usual organic sensibility' greets in solitude the experiences he himself generates. But the escape, the transcendence, is rapidly seen to double back on itself: the higher knowledge proves to be a dream of a reversion to the very reality whose antithesis it was to represent.[45]

---

42 F. Schlegel, 1958, II, 182.
43 F. Schlegel, in ib., II, 318.
44 Leonardo: *The Proportions of the Human Body*, after Vitruvius, pen and ink, *c.* 1492, Accademia, Venice.
45 Catherine Belsey: *Critical Practice*, Routledge 1980, 122.

Appendix

'THE SEA HATH ITS PEARLS'

TRANSLATION OF 'VII. NIGHT IN THE CABIN' BY HENRY
WADSOWRTH LONGFELLOW (1807-82)

The sea hath its pearls,
The heaven hath its stars;
But my heart, my heart,
My heart hath its love.

Great are the sea, and the heaven;
Yet greater is my heart,
And fairer than pearls or stars
Flashes and beams my love.

Thou little, youthful maiden,
Come unto my great heart;
My heart, and the sea and the heaven
Are melting away with love!

XII. PEACE[46]

TRANSLATION OF 'XII. PEACE' BY GEORGE MACDONALD
(1824-1905)

High in heaven the sun was glowing,
White cloud-waves were round him flowing;
The sea was still and grey.
Thinking in dreams, by the helm I lay:
Half waking, half in slumber, then
Saw I Christ, the Saviour of men.
In undulating garments white
He walked in giant shape and height
Over land and sea.
High in the heaven up towered his head;
His hands in blessing forth he spread
Over land and sea.
And for a heart, in his breast
He bore the sun; there did it rest.
The red, flaming heart of the Lord
Out its gracious radiance poured,
Its fair and love-caressing light
With illuminating and warming might
Over land and sea.

Sounds of solemn bells that go
Through the air to and fro,
Drew, like swans in rosy traces,
With soft, solemn, stately graces,
The gliding ship to the green shore--

---

46 Footnote by George Macdonald: I have here used rimes although the original has
none. With notions of translating severer now than when, many years ago, I
attempted this poem, I should not now take such a liberty. In a few other points
also the translation is not quite close enough to please me; but it must stand.

Peopled, for many a century hoar,
By men who dwell at rest in a mighty
Far-spreading and high-towered city.

Oh, wonder of peace, how still was the town!
The hollow tumult had all gone down
Of the babbling and stifling trades;
And through each clean and echoing street
Walked men and women, and youths and maids,
White clothes wearing,
Palm branches bearing;
And ever and always when two did meet,
They gazed with eyes that plain did tell
They understood each other well;
And trembling, in self-renouncement and love,
Each a kiss on the other's forehead laid,
And looked up to the Saviour's sunheart above,
Which, in joyful atoning, its red blood rayed
Down upon all; and the people said,
From hearts with threefold gladness blest,
        Lauded be Jesus Christ!

Bibliography

HEINRICH HEINE

The Complete Poems of Heinrich Heine, tr. Hal Draper, Suhrkamp/ Insel, Boston 1982
The North Sea, tr. Vernon Watkins, Faber 1955
Der romantische Schule, Sämtlichte Werke, vol.3, ed. Klaus Briegleb, Hanser, Munich 1971
Salon II, Hoffmann, 1852
The Works of Heinrich Heine, tr. C.G. Leland et al, Heinemann, I, 432.

ON HEINRICH HEINE

Barker Fairley: Heinrich Heine: An Interpretation, Clarendon Press 1963
Robert C. Holub: Heinrich Heine's Reception of German Grecophilia, Heidelberg 1981
S.S. Pawer: Heine: Buch der Lieder, Arnold 1960
—. Heine, the Tragic Satirist: A Study of the Later Poetry 1827-56, Cambridge University Press 1961
—. Heine's Jewish Comedy: A Study of His Portraits of Jews and Judaism, Clarnedon Press 1983
—. Frankenstein's Island: England and the English in the Writings of Heinrich Heine, Cambridge University Press 1986
Nigel Reeves: Heinrich Heine: Poetry and Politics, Oxford University Press, 1974
Ritchie Robertson: Heine, Peter Halban, 1988
William Ross: Heinrich Heine: Two Studies of His Thought and Feeling, Clarendon Press 1956
Jeffrey L. Samons: Heinrich Heine: The Elusive Poet, Yale University Press, New Haven 1969
—. Heinrich Heine: A Modern Biography, Princeton University Press, 1979

A.I. Sandor: *The Exile of Gods*, Mouton, The Hague, 1967
Israel Tabak: *Judaic Lore in Heine*, John Hopkins Press, Baltimore, 1948

OTHERS

M.H. Abrams: *Natural Supernaturalism: Tradition and Revolution in Romantic Literature*, Norton, New York 1971
—. ed: *English Romantic Poets: Modern Essays in Criticism*, Oxford University Press, New York 1975
Ernst Behler: *German Romantic Literary Theory*, Cambridge University Press 1993
M.B. Benn. *Hölderlin and Pindar*, The Hague, 1962
Ernst Benz: *The Mystical Sources of German Romantic Philosophy*, tr. B. Reynolds & E. Paul, Pickwick, Allison Park 1983
P. Bertaux. *Hölderlin; Essai de biographie intérieure*, Paris, 1936
—. *Le lyrisme mythique de Hölderlin*, Paris, 1936
Henri Clemens Birven: *Novalis, Magus der Romantik*, Schwab, Büdingen 1959
Richard Brinkmann, ed: *Romantik in Deutschland*, Metzler, Stuttgart 1978
Manfred Brown: *The Shape of German Romanticism*, Cornell University Press, Thaca 1979
E.M. Butler. *The Tyranny of Greece Over Germany*, Cambridge University Press, 1935
D. Constantine. *The Significance of Locality in the Poetry of Friedrich Hölderlin*, Modern Humanities Research Association, 1979
—. *Hölderlin*, Oxford University Press, 1988
S. Corngold. *Complex Pleasures: Forms of Feeling in German Literature*, Cambridge University Press, 1998
A. Del Caro. *Hölderlin: The Poetics of Being*, Wayne State University Press, 1991
Hans Eichner: *Friedrich Schlegel*, Twayne, New York 1970
Mircea Eliade: *Shamanism: Archaic Techniques of Ecstasy*, Princeton University Press, New Jersey, 1972
—. *Myths, Dreams and Mysteries*, Harper & Row, New York 1975
—. *Ordeal by Labyrinth*, University of Chicago Press 1984
R.W. Ewton: *The Literary Theory of A.W. Schlegel*, Mouthon, The Hague 1971
Richard Faber: *Novalis: die Phantasie an die Macht*, Metzler, Stuttgart 1970
Walter Feilchenfeld: *Der Einfluss Jacob Böhmes auf Novalis*, Eberia, Berlin 1922
A. Fioretos, ed. *The Solid Letter: Readings of Friedrich Hölderlin*, Stanford University Press, 1999

E. Förster, ed. *The Course of Remembrance and Other Essays on Hölderlin*, Cambridge University Press, 1997

Sara Frierichsmeyer: *The Androgyne in Early German Romanticism: Friedrich Schlegel, Novalis and the Metaphysics of Love*, Bern, New York 1983

M. Froment-Meurice. *Solitudes: From Rimbaud to Heidegger*, State University of New York Press, 1995

J.W. von Goethe. *Goethe's Faust*, tr. Louis Macniece, Faber, London, 1951

—. *Selected Poems* [with Eduard Möricke], tr. C. Middleton, University of Chicago Press, 1972

—. *Selected Poems*, ed. C. Middleton, tr. M. Hamburger et al, 1983

—. *Essays and Letters on Theory*, State University of New York Press, Albany, 1987

—. *The Sorrows of Young Werther*, Penguin, London, 1989

—. *Roman Elegies and Other Poems*, tr. M. Hamburger, Anvil Press Poetry, London, 1996

Curt Grutzmacher: *Novalis und Philippe Otto Runge*, Eidos, Munich 1964

Theodor Haering: *Novalis als Philosoph*, Kohlhammer, Stuttgart 1954

M. Hamburger. *Reason and Energy: Studies in German Literature*, Weidenfeld & Nicolson, 1970

—. *Testimonies: Selected Shorter Prose, 1950-1987*, Carcanet, 1989

—. *The Truth of Poetry*, Anvil Press Poetry, 1996

Bruce Haywood: *The Veil of Imagery: A Study of the Poetic Works of Friedrich von Hardenburg*, Harvard University Press, Cambridge, Mass., 1959

Frederick Heibel: *Novalis: German Poet, European Thinker, Christian Mystic*, AMS, New York 1969

Friedrich Hölderlin. *Complete Works*, ed. N. von Hellingrath *et al*, Berlin, 1923

—. *Hölderlin Sämtliche Werke*, Große Stuttgarter Ausgabe, Stuttgart, 1943-77

—. *Selected Poems*, tr. J.B. Leishman, Hogarth Press, 1954

—. *Hymns and Fragments*, tr. R. Siebruth, Princeton University Press, 1984

—. *Hölderlin Folioheft*, ed. D.E. Sattler & E.,E. George, Frankfurt, 1986

—. *Hyperion and Selected Poems*, ed. E.L. Santer, Continuum, 1992

—. *Poems and Fragments*, tr. M. Hamburger, Anvil Press, 1994

—. *Selected Poems and Fragments*, tr. M. Hamburger, Penguin, 1998

—. *Hölderlin's Songs of Light*, tr. M. Hamburger, ed. J.M. Robinson, Crescent Moon, 2012

Glyn Tegai Hughes: *Romantic German Literature*, Edward Arnold, 1979

L. Kempter. *Hölderlin und die Mythologie*, Zurich, 1929

D.F. Krell. "Nietzsche Hölderlin Empedocles", *Graduate Faculty Philosophy Journal*, 15, 2, 1991

—. *Lunar Voices: Of Tragedy, Poetry, Fiction, and Thought*, Chicago

University Press, 1995

—. *The Recalcitrant Art: Diotima's Letters to Hölderlin and Related Missives,* State University of New York Press, Albany, 2000

Alice Kuzniar: *Delayed Endings: Nonclosure in Novalis and Hölderlin,* University of Georgia Press, Athens 1987

Weston La Barre: *The Ghost Dance,* Allen & Unwin 1972

Philippe Lacoue-Labarthe & Jean-Luc Nancy, eds: *The Literary Absolute: The Theory of Literature in German Romanticism,* State University of New York Press, Albany 1988

G. Lemout. *The Poet as Thinker: Hölderlin in France,* Camden House, 1994

E.C. Mason. *Hölderlin and Goethe,* P. Lang, 1975

Géza von Molnar: *Novalis's Fichte Studies,* Mouton, The Hague 1970

—. *Romantic Vision, Ethical Context: Novalis and Artistic Autonomy,* University of Minnesota Press, Minneapolis 1987

E. Meister. *Prosa, 1931 bis 1979,* Heidelberg, 1989

C. Middleton. *The Poet's Vocation: Letters of Hölderlin, Rimbaud and Hart Crane,* Austin, Texas, c. 1967

M. Montgomery. *Friedrich Hölderlin and the German Neo-Hellenic Movement,* London, 1923

Bruno Müller: *Novalis – der dichter als Mittler,* Lang, Bern 1984

John Neubauer: *Bifocal Vision: Novalis's Philosophy of Nature and Disease,* Chapel Hill 1972

Novalis: *Pollen and Fragments: Selected Poetry and Prose,* tr. Arthur Versluis, Phanes Press, Grand Rapids, 1989

—*Hymns To the Night and Other Selected Writings,* tr. Charles E. Passage, Bobbs-Merrill Company, Indianapolis 1960

—. *Hymns To the Night,* Crescent Moon, 2010

Novalis Schriften. Die Werke Friedrichs von Hardenberg, ed. Richard Samuel, Hans-Joachim Mähl & Gerhard Schulz, Kohlhammer, Stuttgart 1960-88

K.J. Obenauer. *Hölderlin-Novalis,* Jena, 1925

R. Peacock. *Hölderlin,* Methuen, 1973

A. Pellegrini. *Friedrich Hölderlin,* Walter de Gruter, Berlin, 1965

L.S. Salzberger. *Hölderlin,* Cambridge University Press, 1952

E.L. Santer. *Friedrich Hölderlin: Narrative Vigilance and the Poetic Imagination,* New Brunswick, 1986

Nicholas Saul: *History and Poetry in Novalis and in the Tradition of the German Enlightenment,* Institute of Germanic Studies, 1984

Helmut Schanze: *Romantik und Aufklärung, Unterschungen zu Friedrich Schlegel und Novalis,* Carl, Nürnberg 1966

—ed. *Friedrich Schlegel und die Kunstheorie Seiner Zeit,* Wissenschaftliche Buchgesellschaft, Darmstadt 1985

A.W. Schlegel: *Kritische Ausgabe der Verlesungen,* ed. Ernst Behler & Frank Jolles, Schöningen, Paderborn, 1989-

F. Schlegel: *Gespräch über die Poesie, Kritische Friedrich Schlegel Ausgabe,* Schöningh, Paderborn, 1958-

—. *Lucinde and the Fragments,* tr. Peter Firchow, University of Minnesota Press, Minneapolis 1971

A. Seyhan. *Representation and its Discontents: The Critical Legacy of German Romanticism,* University of California Press, Berkeley, 1992

E. Sewell. *The Orphic Voice: Poetry and Natural History,* Routledge, 1961

D. Simpson *et al,* eds. *German Aesthetic and Literary Criticism,* Cambridge University Press, 3 vols, 1984-85

E.L. Stahl. *Hölderlin's Symbolism,* Oxford University Press, 1945

A. Stansfield. *Hölderlin,* Manchester University Press, 1944

P. Szondi. *Hölderlin-Studien,* Insel, Frankfurt, 1967

Ronald Taylor: *The Romantic Tradition in Germany,* Methuen 1970

Ralph Tymms: *German Romanticism,* Methuen 1955

R. Ungar. *Hölderlin's Major Poetry,* Indiana University Press, Bloomington, 1975

—. *Friedrich Hölderlin,* Twayne, 1984

A. Warminksi. *Readings in Interpretation: Hölderlin, Hegel, Heidegger,* University of Minnesota Press, Minneapolis, 1987

K. Wheeler, ed. *German Aesthetic and Literary Criticism, The Romantic Ironists and Goethe,* Cambridge University Press, 1984

Life, Life
Selected Poems

Arseny Tarkovsky

translated and edited by Virginia Rounding

Arseny Tarkovsky is the neglected Russian poet, father of the acclaimed film director
Andrei Tarkovsky. This new book gathers together many of Tarkovsky's most lyrical
and heartfelt poems, in Rounding's clear, new translations. Many of Tarkovsky's poems
appeared in his son's films, such as *Mirror, Stalker, Nostalghia* and *The Sacrifice*.
There is an introduction by Rounding, and a bibliography of both Arseny and
Andrei Tarkovsky.

Bibliography and notes 124pp 3rd ed   ISBN 9781861712660 Hbk ISBN 9781861711144

In the Dim Void

Samuel Beckett's Late Trilogy:
Company, Ill Seen, Ill Said and *Worstward Ho*

by Gregory Johns

This book discusses the luminous beauty and dense, rigorous poetry of Samuel Beckett's late works, *Company, Ill Seen, Ill Said* and *Worstward Ho*. Gregory Johns looks back over Beckett's long writing career, charting the development from the *Molloy-Malone Dies-Unnamable* trilogy through the 'fizzles' of the 1960s to the elegiac lyricism of the *Company* series. Johns compares the trilogy with late plays such as *Ghosts, Footfalls* and *Rockaby.*

Bibliography, notes. Illustrated. 120pp
ISBN 9781861712974 Pbk and ISBN 9781861712608 Hbk
9781861713407 E-book

Beauties, Beasts, and Enchantment

CLASSIC FRENCH FAIRY TALES

Translated and with an Introduction
by Jack Zipes

A collection of 36 classic French fairy tales translated by renowned writer Jack Zipes.
Cinderella, Beauty and the Beast, Sleeping Beauty and *Little Red Riding Hood* are among the
classic fairy tales in this amazing book.
Includes illustrations from fairy tale collections.
Jack Zipes has written and published widely on fairy tales.

'Terrific... a succulent array of 17th and 18th century 'salon' fairy tales'
- *The New York Times Book Review*

'These tales are adventurous, thrilling in a way fairy tales are meant to be... The translation
from the French is modern, happily free of archaic and hyperbolic language... a fine and
sophisticated collection' - *New York Tribune*

'Enjoyable to read... a unique collection of French regional folklore' - *Library Journal*

'Charming stories accompanied by attractive pen-and-ink drawings' - *Chattanooga Times*

Introduction and illustrations   612pp.   ISBN 9781861712510 Pbk   ISBN 9781861713193 Hbk

CRESCENT MOON PUBLISHING

web: www.crmoon.com e-mail: cresmopub@yahoo.co.uk

ARTS, PAINTING, SCULPTURE

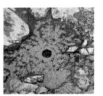

The Art of Andy Goldsworthy
Andy Goldsworthy: Touching Nature
Andy Goldsworthy in Close-Up
Andy Goldsworthy: Pocket Guide
Andy Goldsworthy In America
Land Art: A Complete Guide
The Art of Richard Long
Richard Long: Pocket Guide
Land Art In the UK
Land Art in Close-Up
Land Art In the U.S.A.
Land Art: Pocket Guide
Installation Art in Close-Up
Minimal Art and Artists In the 1960s and After
Colourfield Painting
Land Art DVD, TV documentary

Andy Goldsworthy DVD, TV documentary
The Erotic Object: Sexuality in Sculpture From Prehistory to the Present Day
Sex in Art: Pornography and Pleasure in Painting and Sculpture
Postwar Art
Sacred Gardens: The Garden in Myth, Religion and Art
Glorification: Religious Abstraction in Renaissance and 20th Century Art
Early Netherlandish Painting
Leonardo da Vinci
Piero della Francesca
Giovanni Bellini

Fra Angelico: Art and Religion in the Renaissance
Mark Rothko: The Art of Transcendence
Frank Stella: American Abstract Artist
Jasper Johns
Brice Marden

Alison Wilding: The Embrace of Sculpture
Vincent van Gogh: Visionary Landscapes
Eric Gill: Nuptials of God
Constantin Brancusi: Sculpting the Essence of Things
Max Beckmann
Caravaggio
Gustave Moreau
Egon Schiele: Sex and Death In Purple Stockings
Delizioso Fotografico Fervore: Works In Process 1

Sacro Cuore: Works In Process 2
The Light Eternal: J.M.W. Turner
The Madonna Glorified: Karen Arthurs

LITERATURE

J.R.R. Tolkien: The Books, The Films, The Whole Cultural Phenomenon
J.R.R. Tolkien: Pocket Guide
Tolkien's Heroic Quest
The *Earthsea* Books of Ursula Le Guin
Beauties, Beasts and Enchantment: Classic French Fairy Tales
German Popular Stories by the Brothers Grimm
Philip Pullman and *His Dark Materials*
Sexing Hardy: Thomas Hardy and Feminism
Thomas Hardy's *Tess of the d'Urbervilles*
Thomas Hardy's *Jude the Obscure*
Thomas Hardy: The Tragic Novels
Love and Tragedy: Thomas Hardy
The Poetry of Landscape in Hardy
Wessex Revisited: Thomas Hardy and John Cowper Powys
Wolfgang Iser: Essays and Interviews
Petrarch, Dante and the Troubadours
Maurice Sendak and the Art of Children's Book Illustration
Andrea Dworkin
Cixous, Irigaray, Kristeva: The *Jouissance* of French Feminism
Julia Kristeva: Art, Love, Melancholy, Philosophy, Semiotics and Psychoanalysis
Hélène Cixous I Love You: The *Jouissance* of Writing
Luce Irigaray: Lips, Kissing, and the Politics of Sexual Difference
Peter Redgrove: Here Comes the Flood
Peter Redgrove: Sex-Magic-Poetry-Cornwall
Lawrence Durrell: Between Love and Death, East and West
Love, Culture & Poetry: Lawrence Durrell
Cavafy: Anatomy of a Soul
German Romantic Poetry: Goethe, Novalis, Heine, Hölderlin
Feminism and Shakespeare
Shakespeare: Love, Poetry & Magic
The Passion of D.H. Lawrence
D.H. Lawrence: Symbolic Landscapes
D.H. Lawrence: Infinite Sensual Violence
Rimbaud: Arthur Rimbaud and the Magic of Poetry
The Ecstasies of John Cowper Powys
Sensualism and Mythology: The Wessex Novels of John Cowper Powys
Amorous Life: John Cowper Powys and the Manifestation of Affectivity (H.W. Fawkner)
Postmodern Powys: New Essays on John Cowper Powys (Joe Boulter)
Rethinking Powys: Critical Essays on John Cowper Powys
Paul Bowles & Bernardo Bertolucci
Rainer Maria Rilke
Joseph Conrad: *Heart of Darkness*
In the Dim Void: Samuel Beckett
Samuel Beckett Goes into the Silence
André Gide: Fiction and Fervour
Jackie Collins and the Blockbuster Novel
Blinded By Her Light: The Love-Poetry of Robert Graves
The Passion of Colours: Travels In Mediterranean Lands
Poetic Forms

POETRY

Ursula Le Guin: Walking In Cornwall
Peter Redgrove: Here Comes The Flood
Peter Redgrove: Sex-Magic-Poetry-Cornwall
Dante: Selections From the Vita Nuova
Petrarch, Dante and the Troubadours
William Shakespeare: Sonnets
William Shakespeare: Complete Poems
Blinded By Her Light: The Love-Poetry of Robert Graves
Emily Dickinson: Selected Poems
Emily Brontë: Poems
Thomas Hardy: Selected Poems
Percy Bysshe Shelley: Poems
John Keats: Selected Poems
Joh n Keats: Poems of 1820
D.H. Lawrence: Selected Poems
Edmund Spenser: Poems
Edmund Spenser: Amoretti
John Donne: Poems
Henry Vaughan: Poems
Sir Thomas Wyatt: Poems
Robert Herrick: Selected Poems
Rilke: Space, Essence and Angels in the Poetry of Rainer Maria Rilke
Rainer Maria Rilke: Selected Poems
Friedrich Hölderlin: Selected Poems
Arseny Tarkovsky: Selected Poems
Arthur Rimbaud: Selected Poems
Arthur Rimbaud: A Season in Hell
Arthur Rimbaud and the Magic of Poetry
Novalis: Hymns To the Night
German Romantic Poetry
Paul Verlaine: Selected Poems
Elizaethan Sonnet Cycles
D.J. Enright: By-Blows
Jeremy Reed: Brigitte's Blue Heart
Jeremy Reed: Claudia Schiffer's Red Shoes
Gorgeous Little Orpheus
Radiance: New Poems
Crescent Moon Book of Nature Poetry
Crescent Moon Book of Love Poetry
Crescent Moon Book of Mystical Poetry
Crescent Moon Book of Elizabethan Love Poetry
Crescent Moon Book of Metaphysical Poetry
Crescent Moon Book of Romantic Poetry
Pagan America: New American Poetry

MEDIA, CINEMA, FEMINISM and CULTURAL STUDIES

J.R.R. Tolkien: The Books, The Films, The Whole Cultural Phenomenon
J.R.R. Tolkien: Pocket Guide
The *Lord of the Rings* Movies: Pocket Guide
The Cinema of Hayao Miyazaki
Hayao Miyazaki: *Princess Mononoke*: Pocket Movie Guide
Hayao Miyazaki: *Spirited Away*: Pocket Movie Guide
Tim Burton : Hallowe'en For Hollywood
Ken Russell
Ken Russell: *Tommy*: Pocket Movie Guide
The Ghost Dance: The Origins of Religion
The Peyote Cult

Cixous, Irigaray, Kristeva: The *Jouissance* of French Feminism
Julia Kristeva: Art, Love, Melancholy, Philosophy, Semiotics and Psychoanalysis
Luce Irigaray: Lips, Kissing, and the Politics of Sexual Difference
Hélène Cixous I Love You: The *Jouissance* of Writing
Andrea Dworkin
'Cosmo Woman': The World of Women's Magazines
Women in Pop Music
HomeGround: The Kate Bush Anthology
Discovering the Goddess (Geoffrey Ashe)
The Poetry of Cinema
The Sacred Cinema of Andrei Tarkovsky
Andrei Tarkovsky: Pocket Guide
Andrei Tarkovsky: *Mirror*: Pocket Movie Guide
Andrei Tarkovsky: *The Sacrifice*: Pocket Movie Guide
Walerian Borowczyk: Cinema of Erotic Dreams
Jean-Luc Godard: The Passion of Cinema
Jean-Luc Godard: *Hail Mary*: Pocket Movie Guide
Jean-Luc Godard: *Contempt*: Pocket Movie Guide
Jean-Luc Godard: *Pierrot le Fou*: Pocket Movie Guide
John Hughes and Eighties Cinema
Ferris Bueller's Day Off: Pocket Movie Guide
Jean-Luc Godard: Pocket Guide
The Cinema of Richard Linklater
Liv Tyler: Star In Ascendance
Blade Runner and the Films of Philip K. Dick
Paul Bowles and Bernardo Bertolucci
Media Hell: Radio, TV and the Press
An Open Letter to the BBC
Detonation Britain: Nuclear War in the UK
Feminism and Shakespeare
Wild Zones: Pornography, Art and Feminism
Sex in Art: Pornography and Pleasure in Painting and Sculpture
Sexing Hardy: Thomas Hardy and Feminism

The Light Eternal is a model monograph, an exemplary job. The subject matter of the book is beautifully
organised and dead on beam. (Lawrence Durrell)
It is amazing for me to see my work treated with such passion and respect. (Andrea Dworkin)

CRESCENT MOON PUBLISHING
P.O. Box 1312, Maidstone, Kent, ME14 5XU, Great Britain. www.crmoon.com

cresmopub@yahoo.co.uk   www.crescentmoon.org.uk

CPSIA information can be obtained
at www.ICGtesting.com
Printed in the USA
LVHW082206131021
700394LV00009B/377